WHAT WE WERE
MADE FOR

JB JOSSEY-BASS

WHAT WE WERE MADE FOR

Christian Reflections on Love

Sondra Wheeler

BICENTENNIAL
1807
WILEY
2007
BICENTENNIAL

John Wiley & Sons, Inc.

Library of Congress Cataloging-in-Publication Data

Wheeler, Sondra Ely, 1956-
     What we were made for: Christian reflections on love / by Sondra Wheeler.
        p. cm.—(Enduring questions in Christian life)
     Includes bibliographical references and index.
     ISBN 978-0-7879-7738-2 (alk. paper)
        1. Love—Religious aspects—Christianity. I. Title.
     BV4639.W46 2007
     241'.4—dc22   2006101791

Printed in the United States of America
FIRST EDITION
HB Printing   10 9 8 7 6 5 4 3 2 1

ABOUT THE ENDURING QUESTIONS IN CHRISTIAN LIFE™ SERIES

Enduring Questions in Christian Life™ is a series of books designed to speak intelligently and intelligibly to the deepest spiritual and moral concerns of Christians and thoughtful seekers. The title of the series reflects its purpose: to offer Christian reflection on questions that are significant not just for Christians but for all people. This series seeks to offer thoughtful, compassionate, and provocative explorations of essential matters that arise at the intersection of faith and life. We hope that this series will provide practical guidance for thinking about particular issues in a complex and changing world while opening the reader to a deeper appreciation of the rich direction for life's journey that is available in historic Christian thought. Books in the series seek to be informed by the best in theological reflection, to address enduring questions in new and graceful ways, to avoid polemics, and to jar readers out of old patterns of thinking about life's most significant issues.

Volumes in the Enduring Questions in Christian Life™ Series are designed to speak to those who are unlikely to read (or even find) technical works in Christian theology or ethics but are open to thoughtful reflections that reach both head and heart and help people discern how they are supposed to live this life. The books represent a variety of distinctive faith traditions, but all are ecumenical enough to attract rather than repel seekers and those who come from different strands of

Christian tradition. The Enduring Questions in Christian Life™ Series aims to embody a graceful combination of sober consideration of the human condition and hope in God. Amid the whirl of daily events and the carnage of the daily headlines, the series calls readers into a tradition of Christian reflection that can account adequately both for that carnage and for the hope that gets the last word.

David P. Gushee
Series Editor

CONTENTS

To Gene Outka

Dwight Professor of Philosophy and

Christian Ethics, Yale University

Who taught me that love requires hard thinking

as well as hard work—I am privileged

to call him my friend.

Writing a book about love is a curious experience. On the one hand it has all the aspects of isolation that any writing project involves, at least in the sense that the writer spends long hours alone and thus withdrawn from the basically social character of much of ordinary life. On the other hand, that time is spent thinking entirely about relationships of one sort or another: what they depend on, how they work or fail, and what our experience within them teaches us.

Moreover, like any book, this one is essentially conversational. It is a kind of extended dialogue with many other writers, both known and unknown, living and dead. The writer is also in conversation with a reader, who remains hypothetical but with whom she or he is nevertheless continually concerned. When the task is to make available the richest resources of Christian wisdom about love, then the company the writer gets to keep is particularly excellent, and the work especially rewarding. At the same time, the bar has to be set very high indeed if any sort of justice is to be done to either the sources or the topic. The result is work that is both very hard and unexpectedly sweet.

It is also surprisingly personal. In the pages that follow I do not say a great deal that is autobiographical in any direct sense. Even when I tell stories from my own experience to illustrate a point, it is the point and not the story that is central. But having spent a year thinking about love, I cannot help being conscious of the springs of my own understanding: the relationships as well as the assorted books, conversations, and arguments that have shaped my understanding and my reading of Christian tradition. It therefore seems ungrateful not to acknowledge that background, especially because it inevitably percolates through the reading, thinking, and writing as the work goes on. But where can I begin to acknowledge all that forms me as a person who loves, as well as one who thinks about love?

I found myself thinking about growing up in a home full of affection and the taken-for-granted certainty of being cherished and delighted in. I saw again the images of my father (dead now several years) building us children a tree house in the back yard, and of my mother threatening us unconvincingly with a wooden spoon when we filched from the counter ingredients for the supper she was preparing. It made me aware of how much memory frames what we can believe in and hope for and imitate in our lives, and how far the past reaches into the future.

I remembered teachers as far back as sixth grade who had time for us and challenged us and celebrated with us as we made our way toward adult life, and to whose lives outside of the classroom we never gave a thought. I thought of a friendship stretching through long decades: lost to alcohol for a time and then recovered through my friend's long, perilous road toward sobriety, only to be ended far too soon by a particularly insidious form of cancer. I stopped to appreciate afresh the friends with whom I now share my daily life, their affection and patience, their honesty and faithful prayers, on which I depend.

Reading again the classic Christian texts on love, I thought of the people with whom I had first read them in college and graduate school, and of the happy blend of reverence and critical engagement our teachers had modeled for us. Time and my own experience as a teacher have taught me to prize the remarkable generosity of those professors as they shared with us the fruit of their intelligence and long labor and yet encouraged us to come to our own judgments. (The dedication of this book acknowledges one of those debts.)

And always and inevitably I thought of what I had learned of the long patience and rich fruit of sustained love in the course of my own central relationships: in my marriage of going-on-thirty years, and in caring for the children (now mostly grown) whom I continue to watch with delight and amazement as they emerge smart and funny and full of compassion to engage the world on their own terms. Wisely did our forebears from John Chrysostom to Martin Luther call family life a school for holiness.

By all such gifts and countless others we are prepared to enter into the labors and joys of human love. By them as well we are made ready to know and trust in a Love that goes utterly beyond the reach of our own, bringing forth and sustaining and healing all loves in the end. The list of all those who have loved me and tolerated the many defects in my love for them is long enough, but my debt to them is completely beyond calculation.

INTRODUCTION

Has there has ever been a time and place in which people spent more time talking—and writing, singing, photographing, acting, and filming—about love than our own? You cannot turn on the television or the radio, look at the ads on billboards and buses, glance at the magazines displayed in the grocery check-out line, or wander through the aisles of any book store without being bombarded with the topic. Definitions and advice, checklists and questionnaires, sure-fire methods and brutal de-bunkings ("it's all just biochemistry!") clamor and compete for our attention.

Love means so many things and serves so many functions, from motherhood to marketing, that it has come to seem like a screen on which anything at all can be projected, for any purpose. Much of this stuff is transparent and silly: little cameos of televised intimacy designed to sell instant coffee mix. Some of it is seriously misleading, like all the millions of messages conveyed in our culture which equate love with sex, and encourage us to settle for the latter. No wonder we have become jaded and suspicious.

In fact, we would probably turn away altogether if it were not for one thing: we crave love like we crave air, long for and reach for and hope for it even against all odds and beyond all reason because we must. The quest for love, both to receive it and to bestow it on another, cannot end while we live (though it may be deeply disguised), for in some basic sense love is what we live for. Indeed, it is often the conviction that love is lost beyond recovery that drives people to despair and suicide. But some of the time we stave off despair with illusions, including illusions that are transparent even to us. Where can we look for something better, something both truthful and hopeful? Are there any resources that are well-tested and worthy of trust?

With considerable hesitation I offer more words on this topic about which the supply of words seems so endless and over-whelming. But I am convinced that there *is* wisdom we have lost sight of that could help us if we heeded it. It could help us to understand the depth and the compulsiveness of our searching, and also to understand why it so often goes wrong and fails to satisfy. More important yet, this wisdom could school and guide our basic and universal desire to love and be loved, and so light for us a path into a fuller and more fully human existence. To be truthful, the path is not always easy, and the shape of the love it calls us toward is surprising and sometimes even severe. But it is a path that many others have walked, and by their testimony and by the joyful witness of their lives, we know that it leads home.

Having said something that might sound grandiose, let me admit that there is nothing new in what I will say, nor anything especially original about how I will say it. The insights are culled from the long sweep of Christian tradition and witness. It is drawn from scripture and the deep, deep river of experience and reflection by a long procession of teachers and thinkers, mystics and poets, saints and sinners, some living and some dead.

In a sense, it is there for the taking. But because that inher-itance is complex and does not speak with one voice or even in one language, it is necessary to interpret and select what speaks to our present need. This book can bring these treasures together and offer them in a way that makes their gifts available to those whose daily work does not involve mulling around in the his-tory of Christian thought and practice. Throughout, we will be using this tradition to help us interpret our contemporary struggles to find and offer love, and our examples will come from ordinary folks as well as the saints and heroes of Christian history.

I have gathered this exploration into eight short chapters. Their order is determined by the logic of Christian understandings of love: what it is, and how we know; why and how it so often goes awry; what its healing might require, and what it might make possible. Of course, all such orderings and divisions have a degree of falseness to them, since both our experiences of love and our reflections upon them share a persistent untidiness, and they continually overlap with each other. Still, in this arena we can use all the clarity we can come by. Even a somewhat artificial order will help us see more clearly all the different aspects of what we call by the name 'love', and how they may affect, determine or sometimes thwart one another.

I begin in Chapter One with the love of God, for the one shared conviction of all accounts informed by Christian faith is that God is the source and standard of all genuine loves. Then in Chapter Two I turn to a much more contested matter: To what extent can human beings meet that standard? There I consider such questions as, "Can God's love be returned, or imitated, or directed by us toward others? Does it change our capacities to love, or is it something we as creatures can only passively receive?" In Chapter Three I explore all the things that serve as barriers to human loving. What is it that distorts our loves, or turns them away from the good? What human needs make our love different from God's? More practically, how can things Christians do together help to address those needs, and so help us to love more fully?

This is followed in Chapter Four by a more detailed account of the differences in the kinds of love we experience, from the warmth of settled affection to the fierce protectiveness of parental care to the passion of desire. Here, too, I will talk about the corruptions to which all human loves are vulnerable, and about the particular forms that corruption takes in various kinds of relationships. This in turn brings up an ancient and long-debated issue in Christian thought, the problem of self-love. Without proposing a single proper account of love for oneself, in Chapter Five we will try to come to what we might call (borrowing from philosopher John Rawls) "reflective equilibrium", a balanced view of love for yourself.

Then at last we are in a position to turn to the kinds of every-day relationships we all inhabit, and see what our culling of Christian wisdom about love has brought us in the way of insight and help. We will consider in sequence the love of those nearest to us, our spouses and children (Chapter Six), next the love of friends (Chapter Seven), and finally the love of the neighbors whom we encounter as strangers or enemies (Chapter Eight). This will serve as a test of and a kind of counterweight to our ordinary talk about love, a way of seeing what difference our Christian starting point makes in our understanding and our lives.

Before setting up as guide and interpreter for this deep, rich and various tradition, I must offer one essential caveat. To the extent that I talk not only about what others have taught, but about how we should live in light of their teaching, I speak first and always to myself. I make no claim to being a model of the charity whose character I will explore in the following chapters. Instead, I will be mining the rich ore of our common inheritance in the hope that God, who has given so much wisdom and grace, will use it to bring about a love more like God's own, even in me.

1

God's Love:
The Source and Standard

As we turn to the Christian tradition for help and guidance about love, we must begin with God's love for us. Unanimously (and there is not much in Christianity about which there is unanimity) that tradition teaches that the love of God for us defines love and makes it possible. It is the source of all genuine loves and the standard against which all that calls itself love must be tested. Conversely, our love for God is the center and heart of Christian life, the first goodness from which all other real goods of character and conduct flow. But it is not enough to say that the church universally teaches that the love of God is the wellspring and the touchstone of all true loves. We must also ask, Why is this teaching held to be true, and how does our experience confirm it?

Here the obsession of our popular culture comes to our aid, for we do not have to go far to find evidence that our efforts to give and receive love meet with obstacles and failures at every turn. Novels, movies, and song lyrics are full of the mistakes we make in love and the pain they cause. These stories resonate with us because most of us would have some of the same stories to tell if we were to share them. We love the wrong people, or we love the right ones badly. We find ourselves unable to return the love offered us by another, and we learn that this inability can be as painful as discovering that someone we love does not love us. We both do and suffer wrong in our human relationships. Not only are we deceived by others, mistaking counterfeit loves for the real thing, but we also deceive ourselves. We think we love someone, only to have time show that we mistook who that person really was, or mistook our own temporary neediness for something more enduring.

Even when our loves are truest, most genuine and enduring, we often find that we do not know how to love others well. We grope for the deeds that will nurture and sustain those we love, for the words that will enable them to flourish in and be warmed by our affection. We do not always find them. This is perhaps most famously true in our romantic loves. Their sad tales are told by the high rate of failure in our marriages, and by the fear of marriage expressed by so many young adults who have endured the pain of family dissolution in their childhoods. But it is true as well in our other loves. It is evident in the frustration and grief of parents who find themselves continually at odds with their children, in the chill of friendships that grow weak and strained and dutiful, in the loneliness of those whose relationships are too superficial even for conflict.

To be sure, this is not the whole story. Our loves do not fail us every time or in every respect. I suspect that if they did we would find our lives unbearable. But a person who reaches maturity without significant losses, without fractures and alienations that leave behind a residue of grief and regret, is rare indeed— thus the continuing brisk trade in self-help books that promise to remedy, heal, or prevent our failures at loving.

But healing and prevention are not that easy, for what all these failures represent is a kind of confrontation with ourselves. This confrontation is in part an encounter with our limitations, our honest errors, and our finite resources of insight and wisdom and energy. But it is also a confrontation with darker things. It is true enough that we are imperfect in our understanding and limited in our strength, unable to see into another's heart and only partly acquainted with our own. But we find that we lack not only the wisdom to love well but also the courage to love faithfully when it is hard, costly, or lonely to do so. We are often fearful, driven by the impulse to protect ourselves, and we lack the strength and wholeness that would enable our loves to be free, and freeing to others. To put it more pointedly, our loves are challenged and frequently compromised by a kind of selfishness. Even the need to love and be loved, so basic to our humanity and in one sense the best that is in us, can be fatal. Our very human hunger to be loved can turn devouring.

Grappling with the limits and failures of human loves helps us understand why Christians have always held that it is the love of God that must be the starting point and standard of true love. For God does not share our limitations or our ignorance and is not driven either toward love or away from it by any fear or lack. Knowing us completely and needing nothing from us, God loves us without illusions and without deception, and entirely for our own sake. Thus only God's love is perfectly secure, *unconditional* in a full and unqualified sense. God alone, being supremely free and whole in Godself, can love in perfect liberty, purely out of strength and not weakness.

Surely this utter clarity and purity of motive, this perfectly outward-focused nurture and celebration of another being entirely for her or his own sake, is what we mean by love. At least this is what we *want* to mean and dimly feel we *ought* to mean by it. Yet the chasm between all the various things in ourselves we call love and the wholly unselfish commitment to the well-being of another is wide. In fact, so great is the contrast that some have questioned whether, by this standard, the sorts of passions, attachments, and commitments humans are capable of even deserve to be called love. To the questions surrounding the nature of human and divine love, and to the matter of whether they really are or can be the same sort of thing at all, we will return in the next chapter. For now it is enough to begin at the beginning: to explore what Christian tradition teaches about the centrality of love to God's nature and to the message Christians have to proclaim. Above all, we need to understand what this love has to do with our lives.

STEADFAST MERCY: THE LOVE OF GOD IN HEBREW SCRIPTURE

To explore the love of God we must start with what Christians commonly call the Old Testament, if only to counter a belief that is false but stubbornly persistent: the myth that the God of the

Law and the Prophets is full of wrath and judgment and is to be contrasted with the God of the New Testament, who is gracious and forgiving to the point of being rather a pushover. Of course such a view is altogether at odds with fundamental Christian beliefs: that God is One and that the God who is incarnate in Jesus Christ *is* the God of Abraham, Isaac, and Jacob. But there is an even more basic problem, which is that neither of these contrasting sketches of the character of God bears much resemblance to the way God is represented in the Bible.

In fact, the theme of God's love and its constant expression runs throughout the whole of Hebrew scripture. A variety of Hebrew words are used to name God's loyalty, compassion, and commitment toward the creatures God has made. Two of them in particular (*'aheb* and *hesed*) are frequently translated "love." *'Aheb* is the more general term and it can be used to mean love for God or people or inanimate things. The Hebrew word most commonly used for God's love is *hesed,* which is used only to indicate love toward persons. This word has the flavor of mercy shown to the needy and it connotes love that moves one to rescue. It is therefore sometimes rendered by such words as *faithfulness* or *compassion,* and sometimes by two-word constructions such as "steadfast love," "loving-kindness," or "saving mercy." As is so often the case in translation, there is no true equivalent for *hesed* in English. Still, there can be no doubt that the word captures much of what we mean when we conceive of the love of God as it reaches from the height of power and holiness to human beings in their weakness and need.

The whole of Psalm 136 is a hymn whose refrain is an affirmation of God's *hesed.* Each of its twenty-six verses ends the same way, displaying that merciful love is the very heart of Israel's understanding of God's nature and activity:

> O give thanks to the Lord for he is good, for his
>   steadfast love endures forever. . . .
> to him who by understanding made the heavens,
>   for his steadfast love endures forever;
> It is he who remembered us in our low estate, for his
>   steadfast love endures forever;

and rescued us from our foes, for his steadfast love
    endures forever. . . .
he who gives food to all flesh, for his steadfast love
    endures forever. . . .
O give thanks to the God of heaven, for his steadfast
    love endures forever!
PSALM 136:1,5,23–26 RSV[1]

For the psalmist, the enduring love of God is the framework
within which all divine acts are to be understood. It is love that
brings creation and all its wonders into being (vv. 5–9), and love
that leads Israel out of slavery in Egypt (vv. 11–12). The same love
leads the people through want and danger into a land and a heritage (vv. 13–14, 21–22). Love is the impetus behind God's action
even when that action is violent, as when God strikes down not
only the oppressive Pharaoh (vv. 10, 15) but also other kings who
threaten Israel (vv. 19–20). God's loving-kindness is characterized
by his remembering the lowly who have no other hope and
coming to their rescue (vv. 23–24). But God's loving care extends
beyond the people chosen to be God's own, and indeed beyond
humanity itself. It is manifest in his sustenance of life on the
Earth, for all creatures receive their food from God's hand (v. 25).

Other psalms expand on each of these themes and add many
others. The steadfast love of God is the hope of the righteous
who long for communion with God (Ps. 5:7) and of the sick
who ask God for mercy and help (Ps. 6:4). The love of God is
seen in the defense of the innocent from their enemies (Ps. 17:7)
and celebrated as the sure basis of confidence for those who are
beset with troubles (Ps. 31:21). It is the repentant sinner's assurance of pardon (Ps. 32:10; 51:1), the last refuge against despair for
those drowning in grief (Ps. 57:10), and the final plea of those
staggering under the weight of divine punishment (Ps. 77:7–9).

The same confidence that God is known in enduring love is
shown in the rest of the Old Testament, where it is woven through
narrative, prophecy, and law. In an act poignant for its evocation
of a lost intimacy, God is shown providing for the couple cast out
of Eden, making garments to cover the nakedness that their disobedience has made a matter for shame (Gen. 3:21). Not even

righteous anger at human wickedness can completely overcome
God's compassion, so a way of rescue is provided for humankind
even in the midst of the judgment of the flood (Gen. 6:13–18).
The calling of Israel is expressly attributed to divine love, as God
"sets his heart upon" Israel in her weakness and insignificance
and makes her his own people (Deut. 7:7–8). The giving of the
Law itself is the mark of God's passionate desire to make Israel
a people and to bless them (Deut. 33:3–4).

Even the calls to obedience to God's commands and the dire
threats of suffering and disaster to follow disobedience are understood within the biblical narrative as expressions of love. They
come out of God's passionate desire that the people would
choose the way of life and flourishing (Deut. 30:28). Moreover,
the warnings of the punishment to follow unfaithfulness are
oddly coupled with two predictions. The first is that Israel would
certainly fail to heed those warnings. The second is that when, at
the end of a long, bitter period of sorrow and suffering, Israel
turned again to God, she would be welcomed into a renewed
and deepened covenant. Both predictions are already in view in
the closing pages of Deuteronomy:

> And when all these things come upon you, the blessing and the
> curse, which I have set before you, and you call them to mind
> among all the nations to which the Lord your God has driven
> you; and you return to the Lord your God, you and your chil-
> dren, and obey his voice with all your heart and all your soul:
> then the Lord your God will restore your fortunes, and have
> compassion upon you, and he will gather you again from all
> the peoples. . . . And the Lord your God will circumcise your
> heart and the heart of your offspring, so that you will love the
> Lord your God with all your heart and with all your soul, that
> you may live. [Deut. 30:1–3, 6 RSV]

It is the persistent and tender love of God, often spurned and
disregarded, that binds God to Israel despite her repeated flirta-
tions with other gods and other loves: "How can I give you up,
O Ephraim! How can I hand you over, O Israel! . . . My heart

recoils within me, my compassion grows warm and tender. I will not execute my fierce anger" (Hosea 11:8–9).

But despite God's enduring loyalty to Israel, divine compassion is not limited to the covenant people. The artful story of Jonah highlights God's readiness to forgive even the inhabitants of Nineveh, capital city of Israel's great enemy, Assyria. Jonah, an obscure prophet who counseled king Jeroboam, is called on to deliver news of God's coming judgment upon the city. Instead Jonah flees, boarding a ship for Tarshish so that God must pursue and miraculously return him to shore. Finally Jonah declares the word of the Lord to the city. To Jonah's dismay, Nineveh repents and is spared. Peevishly Jonah complains to God: "This is why I fled to Tarshish; for I knew that you were a gracious God, slow to anger and abounding in steadfast love, and ready to relent from punishing" (Jon. 4:2). So offended is Jonah by God's mercy to the enemy that he sits down in a booth in the wilderness, announcing his intention to wait for death. In a vivid parable, God answers Jonah's anger over the death of a vine God has made to shade him, pointing out that Jonah had not made the vine whose loss he grieves, whereas God has made all the people of Nineveh, "who do not know their right hand from their left," along with all its livestock (Jon. 4:11).

God's sovereignty over all the Earth and its peoples, and the justice of God's judgment of them, is allied with divine compassion for them all. Even the book of Isaiah, written amid the pains of exile and full of excoriations of Israel's enemies, retains this universal vision. In the midst of the alternating pleas, promises, and denunciations that fill its chapters, we can still find predictions that one day even "the nations" will come to know and worship God and be welcomed into fellowship. With this consummation in view, God can call out to "Egypt, my people" and "Assyria, the work of my hands" (Isa. 19:21–25).

The writers of Hebrew scripture used every means at their disposal to convey the breadth and depth, the warmth, and the sheer unshakeable persistence of divine love. This love is variously pictured in poetry and parable, metaphor and story, where it is compared to (and ultimately dwarfs by comparison) the passion of lovers and the tender devotion of mothers. God is the people's eager bridegroom, their faithful husband, their loving father, their devoted shepherd. But love is not always soft. The course of the love between God and humankind is anything but smooth, and the saga is full of failure, abandonment, and rebellion, to which God responds with grief and anger.

A defining moment of Hebrew prophecy is the recognition that the judgments pronounced against Israel's enemies could be brought down on Israel's own head as well. Rebuking those who look to the "day of the Lord" as a time of vindication for Israel and retribution upon her adversaries, Amos declares, "Woe to you who desire the day of the Lord! . . . Is not the day of the Lord darkness and not light, and gloom with no brightness in it? I hate, I despise your feasts, and I take no delight in your solemn assemblies. . . . Take away from me the noise of your songs; to the melody of your harps I will not listen. But let justice roll down like waters, and righteousness like an ever-flowing stream" (Amos 5:18, 21, 23–24 RSV). (Twenty-seven centuries later a modern prophet, Martin Luther King Jr., used these same words to shatter the complacency of another empire secure in the belief that God was on her side, no matter her offenses.)

Similar themes are laced through Isaiah, Jeremiah, Ezekiel, Joel, and Hosea. All of these prophets unite to declare not merely God's wrath against Israel's foes but also God's righteous condemnation of Israel and Judah for the twin offenses of unfaithfulness to God and oppression and indifference toward the poor, including the stranger. The God of Abraham, Isaac, and Jacob is recognized as more than a tribal deity, more than the reliable partisan of Israel, when the requirement of loyalty to God is extended to mercy and equity within the community and to hospitality and justice outside of it.

But it is the genius of Hebrew scripture to place even judgment within love's orbit. *Because* the loving mercy of God is universal in its scope, so must be God's judgment upon evil. God's justice and desire for the flourishing of all God's creatures causes God to condemn and promise the destruction of everything that destroys life, undermines community, and rends the peace and unity of creation.

The jealousy attributed to God in the Law and the Prophets is not, like so much of our own jealousy, an expression of fear and mere possessiveness. It is God's fierce and absolute rejection of all the false gods and false loves that will lead humankind astray and ultimately be death dealing. The life of the world has its source in God, without whom it cannot endure, and the covenant is the framework of faithful and forgiving mutuality that makes human communion with God possible. The second book of that covenant, what Christians have named the New Testament, brings news of the extraordinary lengths to which God has gone to renew and sustain that bond.

LOVE MADE FLESH: THE LOVE OF GOD IN THE NEW TESTAMENT

Even people who know very little of the New Testament are likely to have seen the message "God is love," if only on a bumper sticker on the way to work or on a Sunday school poster in childhood. Because these few words are so often left to stand alone, it is not easy to tell just what they mean or how they might have any bearing on our struggles. They may sound like happy talk, a religious version of "have a nice day"—OK on a Sunday school poster, maybe, but not very helpful in guiding our grown-up lives. But the words are part of a passage from one of the letters of John, where they come as a caution to those who might be tempted to think they are advancing far in the Christian life. Here they are in their original setting:

> Beloved, let us love one another. For love is of God, and everyone that loves is born of God, and knows God. The one who does not love does not know God, for God is love. [1 John 4:7–8 AT]

The historical context of these words makes plain the challenge they offer. Biblical scholars believe this letter was written around the end of the first century after Christ's birth, when the generation that had known Jesus directly was passing or gone. At this time there were several ongoing arguments about who Jesus was, about why he had come, and particularly about how those who belonged to him were supposed to live.[2] Various schools of thought and various teachers were claiming to be the true guides to spiritual maturity. The writer of this letter is sending a message not to one particular person or even to one congregation but to a whole group of churches beset by conflicting directions. He is telling them how they can know the difference between true and false claims about Christian faith and life.

He begins the passage with this warning: "Beloved, do not believe every spirit, but test the spirits to see whether they are from God" (1 John 4:1). First he tells his readers to trust only those who confess that Jesus came in the flesh (4:4). (This is a defense against certain supposedly Christian groups who despised the body and therefore denied that the Son of God could really have taken on flesh.) But because well-sounding words are not enough to identify those who are faithful teachers, he further explains how those who truly know God will behave: they will practice love, because that is what they have received and learned from God.

The author does not content himself with merely saying that those who really know God will be loving. That would suggest that his readers could define the meaning of love to which God conforms, and there were as many pretenders to the title of love in the first century as there are in our own. Instead, he offers a quite concrete and singular definition:

> God's love was revealed among us in this way: God sent his only Son into the world so that we might live through him. In this is love, not that we loved God, but that God loved us, and sent his Son to be the atoning sacrifice for our sins. . . . So we know and believe the love God has for us. God is love, and those who abide in love abide in God, and God abides in them. [4:9–10, 16]

For the writer of 1 John, the coming-in-flesh of God's Son defines love. This is what love looks like and how it is lived out in a world where the communion between God and humankind has been violated and broken. The letter has already made explicit the extremity to which love will go: "By this do we know love, that [Jesus Christ] laid down his life for us . . ." (3:16). This is the ground of Christian confidence and hope: that God's love has been made evident, visible, and utterly unmistakable in Christ, so that we might "know and believe," experience and trust, the depth of God's love.

The love of God, then, is not an idea, nor is it simply a feeling or attitude on God's part. It is an activity, one that leads to the cross. The character of God's love is essentially expressed in this: its readiness to go to any lengths, to the outer limit of self-sacrifice, to restore the relationship that is broken by sin. It is important to note that love undertakes the costly work of reconciliation from God's own side. The initiative comes not from the offenders seeking pardon but from the righteous One, who abandons his just claim in order to heal the breach by taking its fatal consequences upon himself.

It should be easy to recognize that it is *hesed,* the abiding, long-suffering, determined, and unshakeable love of God, that is made flesh in Jesus Christ. Jesus is the embodied form of God's love, and this is the one whom all Christians claim to have met. This is what enables the writer of 1 John to say with such perfect simplicity, "God is love; anyone who does not love, does not know God."

The letters of John offer us the classic biblical expression of self-giving love as at once the nature and the activity of God, and the sure test of anything that claims to reveal God to us. But in the writings of Paul, particularly the letter to the Romans, we find the fullest exploration of how the love of God made known in Christ transforms human existence. The continuity may be hard to see at first. Paul's starting point is the righteous judgment of God upon evil, and upon the wickedness of those who proclaim evil to be good. Speaking of those who have turned away from the knowledge of God, he begins a fairly hair-raising catalog:

> They were filled with every kind of wickedness, evil, covetousness, malice. Full of envy, murder, strife, deceit, craftiness,

they are slanderers, haters of God, insolent, haughty, boastful, inventors of evil, rebellious toward parents, foolish, faithless, heartless, ruthless. They know God's decree, that those who do such things deserve to die—yet they not only do them, but even applaud those who practice them. [Rom. 1:29–32]

The rhetoric is fierce and off-putting. Of course we may find tolerable enough the notion that God will judge the wicked, who (we reassure ourselves) are obviously not us. We may find ourselves, like Israel before us, enjoying a little the expectation that those whose wrongdoing is obvious to us will be punished. Perhaps, like the Pharisee in Luke's story (18:10–14), we may even thank God that we are not like those "others" whom Paul describes.

But just as we are comfortably anticipating (and joining in) the condemnation of these others, Paul's argument takes a stunning turn: "Therefore you have no excuse, whoever you are, when you judge others, for in passing judgment on another you condemn yourself" (Rom. 2:1). It turns out that Paul's point is not to show how the world is divided into those who satisfy God's righteousness and those who do not. Neither is it to reinforce the complacency of those of us who take ourselves to belong to the favored group. It is instead to show that all human beings stand together under the same judgment, condemned by the same standard of God's holiness, judged by our very readiness to see others' sins but not our own. Our real condition is dire:

> All, both Jews and Greeks, are under the power of sin. As it is written, "There is no one who is righteous, not even one. There is no one who has understanding, there is no one who seeks God. All have turned aside; together they have become worthless." [Rom. 3:96–12a]

But Paul does not go to these lengths merely to declare God's judgment upon all evil. Instead he gathers all human beings under a single judgment in order that he may pronounce over all of us God's single verdict of acquittal:

> Since all have sinned and fall short of the glory of God, they are now justified by his grace as a gift, through the redemption which is in Christ Jesus, whom God put forward as the sacrifice of atonement by his blood, to be received through faith. [Rom. 3:23–25a]

For a single-sentence statement of the gospel's central claim, one might do worse. For Paul as for John, the presence of God's love is made manifest by the Incarnation, and its nature is made plain by the Cross.

The outcome of trust in God's mercy offered in Christ is what Paul calls *justification,* peace with God in a restored relationship. The whole balance of the letter to the Romans is occupied with laying out the transforming power of faith in Christ, the way in which it fundamentally changes our relationship with God, with ourselves, and with one another.

The critical thing, and the thing Paul spends much of his time on, is how little, in one sense, any of this has to do with us. It is God's initiative, God's sacrifice, God's work, as faith itself is God's gift and not our accomplishment. The salvation that Paul is at such pains to explicate rests firmly on God's goodness rather than on any goodness of ours, and for that reason it can exclude the two besetting corruptions of all religious life: pride and anxiety.

Our self-satisfaction is excluded, says Paul, by the knowledge that our acceptance by God is a testimony solely to God's forgiving love and the faithfulness of Jesus Christ and is no part of our own doing. "For by grace have you been saved through faith, and this is not your own doing. It is the gift of God, and not the result of works, so that no one may boast" (Eph. 2:8–9).

Also excluded is the endless, anxious wondering that can torment a person who takes God's righteousness seriously. "Have I done enough? Offered enough sacrifices, said enough prayers, done enough good deeds? Have I been sorry enough to make up for all the things I have done? Even all the inward, secret things that no one else even suspects? Have I managed to satisfy God?" Paul's answer to all such anguished self-doubt is that it wholly misplaces the issue. It is not our goodness or even our repentance but rather God's reconciling love that comes first: "God shows his love for us in that while we were still sinners, Christ died for us" (Rom. 5:8).

The result of such an understanding is a striking blend of humility and confidence, and its fruit is joy. Indeed, no one spends more time celebrating the goodness of God and the sure triumph of divine mercy than does Paul. His hymn to the saving power of God's love is unequaled:

> What shall separate us from the love of Christ? Shall tribulation, or distress, or persecution, or famine, or nakedness or peril, or sword? . . . No; in all these things we are more than conquerors through him who loved us. For I am convinced that neither death nor life, nor angels, nor principalities, nor things present, nor things to come, nor powers, nor height, nor depth, nor anything else in all creation, will be able to separate us from the love of God in Christ Jesus our Lord. [Rom. 8:35; 37–39 RSV]

From this standpoint, and perhaps only from here—in this certainty of a love nothing could shake—it is possible to see how we might find the ground of a whole new existence. We might learn to pray without pretense, confident that God who knows and loves us already will not turn away. Secure in an embrace that depends on God's faithfulness rather than our own, it would be possible to bear the whole truth about ourselves. We could come to a genuine self-acceptance, one that rests on God's fully knowing welcome instead of on the futilities of self-deception or on the esteem of the other people we struggle to impress. We could thus give up trying to "clean up our acts" in favor of cleaning up our hearts.

Finally, armed with the humility that comes of truthful self-knowledge and with the confidence of being nevertheless beloved and secure, we might find new resources of patience and compassion, gentleness and forgiveness, to lavish on others. Being the beneficiaries of such a love, rescued and sustained by a grace we can neither merit nor repay, we might begin the long journey toward learning to love as we have been loved. This, then, is why Christians have always insisted that the love of God must be the source and starting point of all human love: God's love teaches us what love is, and makes our loves possible.

FROM GOD'S LOVE TO HUMAN LOVE

In the story the Bible tells, the love of God is the starting point of all human experience. It is God's love we see at work in creation, and God's saving mercy that is the origin of the covenants with Abraham and with Israel. From the beginning God goes before us: calling us into being, lavishing loving attention on us, seeking us out when we wander off, and reaching out to us in mercy before we ever acknowledge our wrongdoing or our need for forgiveness. The experience of God's love, most fully revealed in Jesus Christ, awakens in us an answering love for God, and its first character is gratitude. As 1 John says, "We love because [God] first loved us" (4:19).

But gratitude is not the sum total of our response. We are used to thinking of God's judgment in terms borrowed from law, as debts that require repayment or crimes that exact a punishment, and such language is found in scripture (for example, Matt. 6:12; Rom. 1:22; II Thess. 1:9). But what is accomplished by God's grace is not merely the cancellation of a debt or the remittance of a penalty; it is the restoration of a relationship. Closely allied with the peace of reconciliation with God is the dawning of something we may call adoration. It is the beginning of a kind of pure delight in God's goodness and beauty, the celebration of God's greatness as an object of praise in and for itself.

The effort to give voice to that delight in God fills the psalms, where it is expressed both as longing for God and in hymns about the sweetness of life in God's presence. It brings Paul to the outer limits of what can be said, until he grasps for words and falls silent: "O the depth of the riches and wisdom and knowledge of God! How unsearchable are his judgments, and how inscrutable are his ways" (Rom. 11:33).

Something of the breadth and depth of the response that God's mercy is to call forth in us is expressed already in the first commandment: "You are to love the Lord your God with all your heart, and with all your soul, and with all your might" (Deut. 6:4). Such a love for God is understood as the basis of all goodness in human character and conduct, even as the rejection of God is seen as the root cause of all kinds of evil and corruption. Love is the foundation on which every act of obedience and faithfulness is built, that which makes such acts really good and not merely seemingly good, for without such love even our best acts "profit us nothing" (1 Cor. 13:3 KJV).

But the relationship between God and the human being, for all its intensity and intimacy, does not remain strictly between these two. Just as we love the child of a friend for the friend's sake, so Christians are to embrace all those whom God loves for God's sake. What God has done for us, and the love called forth in response, joins us not only to God but also to one another. In fact, so close is the connection that the writer of 1 John can say with complete confidence, "Those who do not love a brother or sister whom they have seen cannot love God, whom they have not seen" (1 John 4:20).

The authority for this intimate connection between love for God and love for other people is not only in 1 John but also in Jesus' own teaching. When he is asked, "What is the greatest commandment?" Jesus replies by quoting Deuteronomy, that the greatest commandment of all is the command to love God with all your heart and soul and mind and strength (Matt. 22:37). But he says immediately that the next is like it: to love your neighbor as yourself. He concludes by adding, "On these two hang all the Law and the Prophets" (Matt. 22:40).

This saying, which scholars call "the double love command," seems simple and easy to understand, if not easy to obey. But the first suggestion that it is not so easy even to understand comes already in Luke's version of the same story. There the words about loving God and neighbor are placed in the mouth of a teacher of the Law. But hardly are the words out of his mouth when he himself asks, "And who is my neighbor?" (Luke 10:29). The

Gospel writer who recorded this story suggests that the questioner is really just trying to exonerate himself and is not fully sincere. But it is an understandable question.

If we are commanded to love our neighbors as we love ourselves, it becomes a matter of pressing importance to find out the scope and especially the limits of that obligation. Does it apply only to those near at hand? Our families? Those whom we know? Those who share our religion? Our nationality? Just how far does it go? These are very natural, very human questions. That is why Jesus' answer is so powerful, and so disturbing. For instead of answering the question, *Who belongs to the category? To whom do I owe this kind of devotion?* Jesus tells a story—and what a story!

> A man was going down from Jerusalem to Jericho and fell into the hands of robbers, who beat him and stripped him and went away leaving him half dead. Now by chance a priest was going down that same road, and when he saw him, he passed by on the other side. So likewise a Levite, when he came to the place, and saw him he passed by on the other side. But a Samaritan while traveling came near him, and when he saw him he was moved with pity. He went to him and bandaged his wounds, bathing them with oil and wine. Then he put him on his own animal, brought him to an inn, and took care of him. The next day he produced two denarii and gave them to the innkeeper, and said, "Take care of him; and when I come back, I will repay you whatever more you spend." Which of these three do you think was neighbor to the man who fell Into the hands of robbers?" He answered, "The one who showed him kindness." Jesus said, "Go, and do likewise." [Luke: 10:30–37]

The parable we call "The Good Samaritan" is not a story about how to tell where the boundaries are; it is a story about how we go about breaking open the boundaries so that more people come within them. The Samaritan helps a stranger who likely would have despised him as a heretic. (Jews of the time regarded Samaritans as having fallen away from the true religion, as worse than the heathen.)

It is, if you like, a story about how we imitate God by look-ing to reforge connections where they have been broken, even by the other party. It requires that we put ourselves at the disposal of the others whose kinship we reclaim. Like so many of the parables, the conduct it recommends is risky and expensive, and a little outrageous. It is not, one feels sure, what the lawyer was looking for.

And of course it is not what we are looking for either. It is frankly hard to imagine what it would look like to take such a commandment seriously. Are we simply to love as we love our-selves all those whom we encounter in need, including those who would (like the man who fell among thieves) certainly not count us among their neighbors? How? Will a general absence of malice or a weak goodwill be enough? Is a modest generosity—say, the change we happen to have in our pockets—enough? Or are we supposed to put our time and our resources at the service of some stranger's need? How much? For how long? How can this be practical? Jesus cannot be serious!

Except that he seems to be entirely serious. Words like these are found not just in the Gospel of Luke but also in Matthew and Mark, Paul and James, the letters of Peter, and the letter to the Hebrews. To the general command to love the neighbor as the self (cited six times) are added more specific and concrete instruc-tions to love strangers, enemies, and persecutors, as well as concrete directions as to the form that love is to take. (Forgiveness, kindness, forbearance, and generosity are prominent in the description of love's character, and active material provision of food, clothing, and shelter are included.)[3]

The common thread in all these texts is that we are to offer to others what God has shown toward us: a generous and active care that reaches across barriers and offenses and takes on itself the task of reconciliation, even where we are the offended party. The rationale for all this is simple: the world has been loved by God as an enemy. Indeed, *we* have been loved even when we have made ourselves and remained the enemies of God, for "while we were enemies we were reconciled to God through the death of his son" (Rom. 5:10). It is the love of God that reaches out to rescue us, and we testify to and celebrate and make visible that love in this one fundamental way: by imitation. Therefore Jesus says, "If you love those who love you, what credit is that to you? For even sinners love those who love them. And if you do good to those who do good to you, what credit is that to you? For even sinners do the same. . . . But love your enemies, and do good . . . and your reward will be great, and you will be children of the Most High, for he is kind to the ungrateful and the wicked" (Luke 6:32, 35).

But we are not quite finished. While we are still trying to absorb the suggestion that God calls us to put our time and money and energy at the disposal of even our enemies, the final penny drops. The first letter of John is where we find the classic expression of the nature of God as love. It is also where the extraordinary price of God's love is made perfectly explicit and put forward as the model for the love we are commanded to show toward one another.

This chapter earlier quoted the beginning of 1 John 3:16. Here it is in its entirety: "By this we know love, that [the Son] laid down his life for us; and we ought to lay down our lives for the brothers and sisters." This, then, is the ultimate standard, that those who know God keep his commandments, which are "that we should believe in the name of his Son Jesus Christ, and that we love one another as he has loved us"—that is, all the way to sacrifice. How can we take seriously demands as radical and even terrifying as these?

It may be some help to recognize that they are not really presented as demands at all. They are instead proclamations of what God in Jesus Christ has done and made possible, for this is where John's letter begins. God has broken into a world lost in rebellion and isolation, enslaved by the inevitability of death and the fear of judgment, and reclaimed its territory as God's own. God, "in whom there is no darkness at all" (1 John 1:5), is faithful as well as just (1:9) and offers to cleanse of unrighteousness all who turn to God so that they may dwell with God in holy joy.

The shape of our embracing of that extraordinary offer is simply this: that in response to the extravagance of God's love we might begin to love those who share it with us. This is not a *rule* for obtaining life with God, like a ticket you must produce to get in the door. It is the *character* of a life shared with the God who is love. It is not a requirement as much as it is an invitation, for love, after all, is the very heart of the flourishing for which God made the world. But even with all that said, it would be absurd not to acknowledge that the possibility seems remote: Can we learn to love as God loves? Can we even want to?

In the next chapter we return to the problem we skirted earlier, of what kind of love we can believe ourselves capable of and whether there is any hope of our obeying the command to love God and our neighbor.

Can We Measure Up?

T here is a story told about St. John, traditional author of the fourth Gospel and the three short letters bearing his name. When he had grown very old and weak and his community was sure that death was approaching, attendants were appointed to keep constant watch by his bed. They were given strict instructions to record any final teaching so that it might be preserved and treasured by the Church. All the listeners paid close attention and wrote down every word they heard John utter. When their vigil was ended and the old saint had finally died, they compared what they had written. Over their weeks of watching, all had recorded only the same three words: "Love one another."

As we saw in Chapter One, the merciful kindness of God is so central to God's very being that "God is love" can serve as the climax of John's message. This is a word of such deep reassurance that many saints and mystics have passed years on end meditating on its richness. There is also a sense of fittingness, even inevitability, to the idea that John and even Jesus himself join to it: that those who know God, knowing love, will be gripped by it, drawn up into it, and in some way transformed. They will respond to love *in* love, reaching upward toward God and outward toward the other human beings they encounter.

This just feels right to us, so that even those who profess no religious faith of their own recoil when they see those who say they know God acting arrogantly, with malice or contempt. This,

we think, is not what they have learned from the One they claim
to worship. The contradictions of faith and hatred make religiously inspired wars particularly tragic, and religiously motivated
violence especially terrible and perplexing. We are persuaded
when we read the words of John's letter: "Whoever does not love
does not know God, for God is love" (1 John 4:8), and "those
who say 'I love God' and hate their brothers or sisters are liars"
(1 John 4:20).

But there are problems with taking love as the touchstone of
Christian existence. First, it is hard to square with what we see.
Anyone who has been involved in the life of a church knows that
it is just not true that everyone who claims to love God displays
the marks of love in their conduct toward others. Of course one
may conclude (as the first letter of John seems to, at least in part)
that this just proves that not everyone who claims to know God
does so in fact! But the matter is not quite so simple. The writer
of 1 John can still speak of sin within the Christian community.
Indeed, he says, "if we say we have no sin we make him a liar and
his word is not in us" (1:10 RSV), and that sin continues to make
its presence felt. Even in the relationships that claim to have love
as their basis there is often a great contrast between the patience,
the unselfishness, the enduring faithfulness of God's love and the
fleeting, shallow, patently self-serving character of much of what
goes by the same name between human beings.

We have testimony to the messy and complicated business of
human response to God's love even in Paul. He is the world's best
known Christian convert, Apostle to the Gentiles, certainly the
central theologian of the New Testament. Yet in a famous passage
he expresses pain and perplexity at his own conduct: "I do not do
the good that I want, but the evil I do not want is what I do. . . .
Wretched man that I am! Who will deliver me from this body of
death?" (Rom.7:19, 24 RSV). Of course part of Paul's point here
is to celebrate the victory over evil given to us in Jesus Christ.
But nevertheless there are in Paul, as elsewhere in scripture, signs
of the continuing struggle, the far-from-complete transformation of a heart touched by the love of God.

In addition to these problems we observe, there are what we
might call conceptual problems. There are many reasons to ques-

tion whether God's love for us is something to which we *can* respond in kind, and what it would mean, exactly, to do so. After all, there are dramatic and permanent contrasts between God as a lover of human beings and us—our nature and capacities. And the difference is not just a matter of degree, as if God were simply a bigger and better version of us: it is a basic difference in kind. In whatever way we may be sought out by God, drawn into relationship by divine mercy, the gulf between creature and Creator remains vast.

God is eternal and infinite, while we are mortal and limited entirely within time and space. God is holy, goodness itself, in whom there is no darkness or weakness or wavering. By contrast, we find ourselves unable to meet with complete consistency even the basic standards of honesty, fairness, and self-restraint we set for ourselves. God is the very cradle of being, the One in whom all creation lives and moves and has its existence. We, meanwhile, are contingent through and through. We depend on a whole series of physical circumstances, from the small range of temperatures our bodies will tolerate to the working of complex physiological processes whose brief interruption will end our lives. Beyond our physical requirements, our psychological survival and even our understanding of ourselves as human beings depends on other people affirming and responding to us, as our spiritual lives depend on our being sustained and forgiven by God.

Our limitations and our fundamental and continual neediness form part of the backdrop to all our perceiving and acting and desiring—including our recognizing or turning toward God. Part of how we know God's love for us is that God is attentive and gracious in meeting our needs. But one of the things we affirm about God is that this One needs nothing and depends on nothing outside of God. The deity, whom Christians conceive as the divine community of the Trinity, is perfect and complete, without lack or need, without defect or fault. In what way, then, can we love God? How can we even imitate God's love in relation to each other when we have, so to speak, so little in common with our divine model? It is easy for us to wonder whether the New Testament writers, for all their eloquence and appeal, are just aiming too high for us.

Because love is central to everything Christians believe both about God and about Christian life, it is not surprising that there has been a great deal of reflection on these questions across the two thousand years of Christian history. Some of it is ancient, going back to the third- and fourth-century writers we call the church fathers. Some arises out of the practices and reflections of monastic communities, ancient and modern. Some comes from the poetic and visionary writings of mystics and saints of earlier centuries. More recently there is a whole academic and philosophical literature analyzing and debating the nature of God's love for humanity and the possibilities of human love for God and one another.

Some of this stuff is dry and much of it is difficult to read. As a result, it is little known even among thoughtful and educated Christians. But the matters examined are not just of technical interest to historians, theologians, and philosophers. They are important to everyone, because the kind of love we think human beings are capable of shapes how we act. Having an effect on what we believe, it also affects what we can hope for, and pray for, and practice in our lives. In the remainder of this chapter I draw on an eclectic sampling of these sources to help shed light on our basic question: *If God's love is the standard, can we hope to meet it?*

LEARNING FROM OUR FORBEARS

The earliest generations of Christians living after the New Testament took its words about the importance and practical shape of love with full and sometimes amazing seriousness. Among the surviving documents of the Roman imperial bureaucracy is a letter written by a Roman official complaining about the difficulties he is having with suppressing the pesky Christian sect in his area. He says it is hard to keep people from joining the Christians because they take such good care of one another and even of outsiders. He writes that they not only feed their own poor, but they even feed the poor among their frankly pagan neighbors. The beleaguered official reports that when one of the Christians is sent to labor in the salt mines as punishment, several of his fellows will voluntarily go along with him to keep up his spirits! What is one to do with such people, he wonders?

But despite such testimonies, the early Church was not unaware of, or immune to, the challenges of wholeheartedly loving God and neighbor. Like us, they found it hard to resist the busyness, competition, and self-absorption of commerce and the anxieties and frustrations of family life. These preoccupations competed for their attention and chipped away at their efforts to live a life centered in Christian love. Within a few generations, movements were born within the Church that sought to purify and renew the wellsprings of its life and holiness. These movements began with individuals like St. Anthony of Egypt going out into the desert to pursue a closer communion with God in solitude. These solitary seekers attracted other individual men and women who learned from their teaching and adopted their form of life. Still others gathered into little communities that fashioned a common pattern of life, work, and worship in order to attain a greater degree of holiness.

In some ways, these long-ago ancestors of the Church are hard for us to understand. Some of their practices, such as the extremes of self-deprivation and physical discipline that some of them followed, strike us as strange or even destructive. But it is clear from the writings they left behind that even their practices of self-denial were not understood by them as good in themselves and were not undertaken for the sake of the suffering they might involve. They were intended to free these men and women from distractions and passions that got in the way of loving God and neighbor with undivided hearts.

Human desire for pleasure and ease and for the praise and approval of others were not thought by these early Christians to be evil in themselves. But it was their observation that such natural impulses and longings were often at war with the demands of love. Those who set out to love God "with all their hearts and all their minds and all their strength, and their neighbors as themselves," who wanted to "be perfect" as Jesus had bidden them to be, adopted a form of life designed to bring everything else into subjection to this one overriding goal. This was the aim of all their disciplines.

Among the collection of stories told about these early monks is one that illustrates this point:

> Saint Epiphanius sent someone to Abba Hilarion with this request: "Come, let us see one another before we depart from the body." When he came, they rejoiced in each other's company. During their meal, they were brought a fowl. Epiphanuis took it and gave some to Hilarion. [Hilarion] said, "Forgive me, but since I took the habit, I have never eaten meat." Then [Epiphanius] answered, "Since I took the habit, I have not allowed anyone to go to sleep with a complaint against me, nor have I gone to sleep with a complaint against anyone." [Hilarion] replied, "Forgive me: your discipline is better than mine."[1]

The monastic communities that have come down into our own day have the same basic aims. Even though none of them embraces the extremes of bodily discipline that some of the desert mothers and fathers of the early centuries practiced, nevertheless they exist in order to form people who are able to love more nearly as they have been loved by God. They remind us of something that modern people may need to hear again: love is hard, at least some of the time, and becoming able to respond to the love of God *in* love is a lifelong work that requires real transformation.

Thomas Merton, twentieth-century writer and contemplative monk, speaks of the heart of prayer as "an act of pure love," aimed at becoming "one spirit with Christ in the furnace of contemplation." This, he insists, is at once easy and natural, and profoundly hard, for it requires the destruction of what Merton calls the false "I."[2] This is the self that seeks control and domination and sees the world in terms of the fulfillment of desire, viewing everything in relation to the self. Philosopher Iris Murdoch used a memorable phrase to describe that "false I": she spoke of "the fat, relentless ego." This phrase has become famous because it captures something most people recognize when they stop to think about it: that we rarely lose sight of our own fulfillment for an instant, and it is the nature of our desires never to be satisfied.

Although this is a theme that runs through many religions, it is not just some otherworldly, "spiritual" idea. Every economist, sociologist, and advertising executive knows it. If affluence rises, so does expectation, so people feel no more satisfied than they did before. Even someone who wins ten million dollars in the lottery quickly becomes accustomed to a new standard of living and feels no better off than before.[3] The fulfillment of desire does not quiet desire but stimulates it, which is why advertising continues to work no matter how many things are already stuffed into our closets.

And it is not just in material things that our wanting is endless. Our desires for praise, affirmation, esteem, and affection are likewise practically infinite. Such desires are always at work in us, and they continually challenge our ability to love by tempting us to see and respond to other people primarily in relation to our own needs. Of course it is no great revelation to say that human beings tend to be self-centered and self-absorbed. But we have not always taken that fact seriously enough or acknowledged how much that tendency is at work in all our relationships, even those that are closest.

For example, in the Victorian era, when modern industrial economies were emerging, it was part of popular wisdom to contrast the public world of commerce and politics, full of self-interest and competition and ruthlessness, with the world of home and family. Home was the sphere in which love and loyalty reigned; it was to be, in the phrase of the period, "a haven in a heartless world."[4] (It was also to be presided over by the woman as domestic icon and guardian of all things gentle and soft. Clearly this was a set of ideas with important social and political functions, including keeping women in their proper place. But that is another book!)

In the popular literature of the time, family affection was represented as holy and pure, being somehow preserved from the forces and motives that made public life corrupt. There was a fair amount of sentimentality and self-deception in all this, and some of its descriptions of domestic life make one wonder whether these writers ever really spent time at home. (Of course, such attitudes are not completely gone from the way we think and talk about family life even now, as a trip down any greeting card aisle will show.) But with the end of the century came a reaction against the Victorian picture of family relationships. The reaction had secular forms, like Sigmund Freud's analysis of the hidden dynamics of family life, but it also affected religious thought.

A number of Christian theologians called dramatically into question the natural loves of family and friends. They found in them plenty of evidence of competition and self-interest, and saw more contrast than continuity with the love God offers and commands. In the end, I will argue, they went too far. Their ideal of love was inhuman and finally at odds with the tradition they were seeking to preserve. Nevertheless, they had a genuine point, one we need to take seriously if we are to learn what Christian faith has to contribute to our understanding and practice of love.

To make that point clear, I outline here the ideas of Anders Nygren, a Lutheran theologian writing early in the twentieth century. His work represents one end of a spectrum of judgments about what we should look for or hope for in human loves. It is important partly because it stimulated a great deal of later discussion, but it is also useful to us because it highlights a central set of questions: What are human beings capable of, and what do our loves have to do with the love of God?

LOVES AT WAR

Nygren sets out to explain and clarify the conception of Christian love, which he calls by the Greek word *agape* to distinguish it from other things we call love.[5] He believes that the purity of this idea is gravely threatened by another form of love, with which it has become confused in the course of history. That other form of love is what he calls *eros,* likewise a Greek word whose ordinary meaning is related to romantic and sexual love.

What is distinctive about Nygren's work, and what has prompted intense discussion and controversy in reaction, is his insistence that *agape* and *eros* are not merely distinct forms of love but are in fact polar opposites. Where *agape* reaches out to another purely for the other person's sake, erotic love is simply the longing to possess, enjoy, and finally incorporate whatever fulfills the lover. It is essentially self-seeking. It loves its object always as a source of delight, satisfaction, and flourishing *for the lover.* While *agape* is fundamentally self-giving, *eros* is fundamentally selfish. In Nygren's view, *eros* and *agape* utterly contradict each other, so the only true choice in relation to them is either–or.

The love of God is, of course, the source and model for *agape,* and Nygren describes this love as spontaneous, unmotivated, and creative. It springs entirely from God's nature rather than being called forth as a response to something in the world outside. Nygren insists that God does not love human beings (or indeed any creatures) because they have some sort of intrinsic goodness or value that God recognizes and honors. Rather, the spontaneous love of God *creates* value in whatever God loves.

And this is the root of the difficulty, for this is not a model we can imitate. Because God is the initiator of relationship with human beings, our love for God can never be spontaneous; it must always be responsive. Furthermore, human love for God is entirely accounted for by the love and mercy God has shown toward us, so it cannot be without motive. Finally, human love certainly cannot create value in God; it can only respond to God's goodness. Nygren reaches the inevitable conclusion: human beings cannot really love God as God loves them.

But he also denies the possibility that our love for each other can really reflect God's love. This is because, according to Nygren, all human loves are "erotic" (in his broad sense) at their very core. We look to others and are drawn to them because in some way they complete us, satisfying our longings, offering us delight, or easing our loneliness. This is easy to see in the loves that include dependence, such as a baby's love for the mother who feeds and cares for her. But Nygren is convinced that it is actually true of every form of human relationship.

Our loves are really always about the pursuit of our desires, the fulfillment of our needs, and as desiring loves they are always really egocentric, a complex form of self-love. Human loves, he says, are aptly called self-serving. As lovers in their own right, human beings are simply incapable of being genuinely *for the other.* They are therefore unable to imitate the outreaching love of God, which does not go looking for goodness or delight or the satisfaction of need but is wholly and simply self-giving. Human beings cannot, it seems, obey Jesus' command to "love one another as I have loved you."

Nygren's response is to give an interpretation of Christian love of neighbor that makes it entirely and solely dependent upon God. Convinced that human love cannot be true *agape* because of its captivity to self-interest, he ends up speaking of human beings simply as "means" or "extensions" of God's own love. Christians are to be filled up by the spontaneous, unmotivated, creative love of God to such an extent that God's love washes through them to their neighbors. "In the life that is governed by *agape,*" he says, "the acting subject is not man himself; it is God. . . . The Christian has nothing of his own to give, and the love which he shows to his neighbor is the love which God has infused into him."[6]

WHAT WE CAN LEARN HERE

Over the seventy-five years since its initial publication, readers have found Nygren's work both powerful and troubling. To his credit, he shines a brilliant light on how God's love, shown above all else in the cross of Jesus Christ, seeks us out in an act of complete freedom and grace. Jesus offers himself to us and claims us as his own, and the ground for both is nothing we can do or fail to do but rather God's own nature as love, reaching across the barriers that divide us from God's holiness.

Such a standard for love forces us to look more deeply and critically at human relationships. If the model to be imitated is God's patient love for enemies, then such things as our expected mutual exchanges of kindness with friends and even our routine caretaking within our own families offer only the palest possible image of it. If as Christians our love for our neighbors is to serve as a sign of God's love for humankind, then it must be broader, more vigorous, more encompassing by far than these ordinary and reciprocal affections.

What's more, if the measure of love is "laying down our lives," then much of what passes for love among us is unmasked as something else: as the pursuit of our own benefit, the satisfaction of our own needs, the seeking of our own good. How much this indictment may stick is suggested by the fragility of so many of our relationships, even those that include explicit promises and lasting obligations. When needs go unmet or satisfactions fade and the burdens of a relationship outweigh its benefits, then commitments to spouses and children, to friends and communities, to shared tasks and goals, are likely to be abandoned as we seek our own fulfillment elsewhere.

Worst of all, in the midst of such failures we are often both self-deceiving and self-excusing. "We have done the best we can," we tell ourselves; "it just didn't work out." Our newspapers, our courtrooms, our office coffee breaks, our conversations with friends, and unhappily often our own lives are full of these stories. Loves are undertaken, commitments are made, trusts are given, and bonds are forged, only to be left behind when the price of maintaining them rises too high.

But despite its powerful insights, Nygren's proposal has serious problems. First, his picture of *agape* gives us a model that seems to make human love for God and neighbor, strictly speaking, impossible. This conclusion flies in the face of central biblical commands. Further, his understanding of love as "creating value" rather than responding to it may be appropriate to God, but it cannot be appropriate to any love humans might have for God or one another. Finally, by insisting on an absolute purity of motive, an inhuman absence of need or self-concern, Nygren leaves us with an understanding of Christian love in which we seem to be only bystanders. We can be recipients of God's love, perhaps even channels of it, but we cannot really be subjects of such a love. The result is that all we mean by love is put aside as (at best) irrelevant to Christian love and (at worst) incompatible with it.

The other problem with Nygren's analysis is that it cannot make sense of the examples of dedicated and costly love which human beings also offer. Most of us know of such examples—relationships faithfully sustained despite real hardship, devoted service to people and purposes that belie his depressing account. Parents more often than not display a deep loyalty to their children, and an afternoon spent in a children's cancer ward offers heartbreaking evidence of how much suffering they will bear for love. Most of the day-to-day care of the elderly and sick in this country is still provided for free by their relatives, many of whom are also elderly with health problems of their own. And such service is not always reserved for later in life. A recent article in the *Washington Post* tells one such story, profiling a husband who cares for his progressively more disabled wife. His fatigue and sorrow are evident in his face and in the story he tells—but so is his matter-of-fact commitment to her well-being and her happiness at being at home. He will care for her gladly for as long as he is able.

Nor is such loving service confined to families. I personally know doctors who work long hours for minimal pay or none giving care to the poor and homeless in my own city of Washington. I have seen pastors who do everything from roof repair to posting bond money in the middle of the night in service to their struggling congregations. The fact is, despite what one of my teachers called "our frequently dismal moral performance," we human beings are not consistently bad enough for Nygren's account to be the whole truth.

Even so, it is impossible to deny that Nygren's austere analysis has some truth to it. This remains a world where public and private trusts are routinely betrayed. Business leaders and politicians are commonly indicted, divorce rates remain high, and clergy are found to have abused and exploited those in their care. The dim expectations arising from the account of human attachments as fundamentally selfish, and the biting assessments of human claims to love, have been shared by many other thinkers. They include some of the twentieth century's best known and most eloquent theologians, some of whom draw upon Nygren directly.

One of the most widely known and influential of these is Dietrich Bonhoeffer, pastor and theologian of the Confessing Church in Germany in the 1930s and 1940s. A brief look at his writing on the subject of love will help us see how a sober and deeply critical appraisal of human loving might still lead to practical conclusions different from Nygren's.

LOVE SUBJECT TO THE TRUTH

Bonhoeffer was brought up in a large, affectionate family and his letters are full of fond recollections of family and friends, of learning and making music in a warm and loving home. His gifts and calling were recognized early and he completed his graduate education at Tübingen at the age of twenty-one. Bonhoeffer served as a pastor and teacher between 1928 and 1933 in a variety of settings both at home and abroad. Meanwhile, he watched with dismay the rise of the Third Reich and the German church's complacent, even cooperative response.

In 1934 he became one of the founders of the German Confessing Church, which opposed the Nazi regime as idolatrous in its claims. By 1939 Bonhoeffer, along with his brother Klaus, his sister Christel, and his brother-in-law Hans von Dohnányi, had become active in the German resistance to Hitler. Dohnányi and Bonhoeffer were arrested in April 1943 and held in a variety of prisons and concentration camps until April 1945, when both were executed at Flossenbürg. The executions of Dietrich's brother Klaus and another brother-in-law followed within a few weeks.

The preceding outline is accurate as far as it goes, but it does not indicate much of what has made Bonhoeffer so influential in the decades since his death. His was a thoughtful, eloquent, relentlessly honest intelligence. Along with the witness of his personal courage, he left behind a legacy of powerful books as testimony to his struggle to see truthfully and live faithfully. Among them is a short but compelling book on Christian community called *Life Together*[7] penned while he directed an illegal seminary subsequently shut down by the Gestapo. Given what we know of his warm personal relationships, this book comes as something of a surprise, for in it he writes of the dramatic opposition between what he calls human and spiritual love.

But judgments about what human beings are like and what they are capable of are not made solely on the basis of our experience in personal relationships. Perhaps it is not surprising that Bonhoeffer wrestled so deeply with the nature of human attachments and the true character of human loves. After all, he had seen love of country used to launch a campaign to dominate Europe. He had heard love of family used as a rationale for the most obscene brutality to those who were thought to represent a threat to the purity of the German race. Finally, he had watched as the German church let its love for homeland and *Volk* (people or kindred) triumph over its loyalty to Christ and his gospel. Bonhoeffer knew that human loves could turn destructive, even demonic, unless they were brought into subjection to the gospel.

Therefore, Bonhoeffer proceeds to draw the sharpest possible contrast between spiritual communities, which are founded upon what God has done for us all in common, and all human communities, which are built upon other connections or attractions between persons. Without Christ, certainly, we could not know or come to God. But also, he insists, without Christ we cannot know our brother, or come to him *as* a brother: "The way is blocked by our own ego."[8]

This is because the only alternative to the spiritual love that binds us to one another through Christ is our human loves. These, Bonhoeffer claims, are based on "the dark, turbid urges and desires of the human mind."[9] A little later he puts it in the same language as Nygren did: "In the community of the Holy Spirit there burns the bright love of brotherly service, of *agape*. In human community of spirit, there glows the dark love of good and evil desire, *eros.*"[10]

We must not misinterpret Bonhoeffer here. He is not talking about *eros* in the sense of sexual desire that is merely pretending to be friendship or warm affection. He is talking about the real thing, what he calls "the human love of one's neighbor."[11]

Such a love may be quite genuine, in one sense. It may even be capable, as he says, of "prodigious sacrifices." But it is not able to sacrifice the love itself, the desired relationship with the beloved. To love as a human being is not to serve the other but rather to desire him or her: "it loves him not as a free person but one whom it binds to himself." It wants "to gain, to capture by every means," for it "desires the other person, his answering love, [and so] it does not serve him."[12] Twentieth-century publisher Margaret Anderson captures the spirit of this claim perfectly in a famous quip: "In real love, you want the other person's good; in romantic love, you just want the other person."

Like Nygren, Bonhoeffer believes that, in this sense of "just wanting the other person," all human attachments have the same basic character. Human loves are unmasked for what they are, *eros* rather than *agape,* when love requires renunciation or when it is rejected by the other person. When human love cannot have the union it longs for, Bonhoeffer charges, it turns into hatred. Human love cannot surrender itself, nor can it love the enemy who refuses to be won over, for both of these involve giving up the goal of union toward which it reaches.

Such a description may seem more plausible if we consider concrete examples. Think of a would-be lover who is rejected and becomes enraged, or of a parent who knows he cannot care for his child but refuses to give her up for adoption. Consider how a man is likely to behave if he falls in love with a woman who is happily married to another man, or imagine that your closest friend comes to you full of enthusiasm for a remarkable new job opportunity—on the other side of the Atlantic!

What do we do when loyalty to "the other person's good" conflicts with our desire for the presence, the enjoyment, the answering love of the person? Conversely, how do we respond when our overtures toward reconciliation with an adversary are harshly turned aside? Bonhoeffer insists that only spiritual love, love that flows from and through Christ as the Mediator between human beings, can hand over the beloved to God. Only such a love allows us faithfully to love someone whom we may not be permitted to enjoy, or an enemy who may never respond.

Up to this point we seem to have an account that sounds very much like Nygren's own, right down to the language of *eros* and *agape*. It seems to suggest a fundamental opposition in which human loves must be overcome and rejected so that spiritual love alone can rule. But in fact Bonhoeffer draws back from such a conclusion. Oddly enough he does so without seeming entirely to notice. What keeps Bonhoeffer from joining in the stern and consistent either-or of Nygren's account of human and Christian love is his attention to actual human relationships, the ordinary contexts in which people come to know and love each another.

Ironically, the first hint that human and spiritual love cannot be conceived of as absolute alternatives to each other comes when Bonhoeffer speaks of dissolving a relationship for the sake of love. His point is that we do not necessarily recognize what true love requires. While we naturally desire the presence and affection of those we love, it may be that what a person we love really needs is separation from us, something Bonhoeffer faces resolutely: "[W]here [Christ's] truth bids me dissolve a fellowship for love's sake, there I will dissolve it, despite all the protests of my human love."[13] In this example, the desired union toward which human love aims is surrendered, "dissolved" for the sake of the truth. But Bonhoeffer is equally clear that human love is present, and it does feel and protest its loss. For the first time it becomes clear that a single human relationship might *include* both human and spiritual love, both the bond in and through Christ, and the ordinary stuff of human attachment.

A little later Bonhoeffer even suggests that relationships in which human and spiritual bonds are mingled are more natural and safer than those which are purely spiritual. In the mixed relationships of ordinary life we are in less danger of confusing the objective, God-given reality of our union in Christ with our human longing for intimacy and immediacy with each other. The presence of that longing is clear, and so are its limits. The everydayness of such relationships, in a sense, is their salvation: "A marriage, a family, a friendship, is quite conscious of the limits of its community-building power; such relationships know very well where the human element stops and the spiritual begins."[14] It is when we imagine ourselves to be in some kind of pure, supernatural communion that we are likely to confuse our own attachments for the work and will of God.

So Bonhoeffer takes for granted that human connections will ordinarily (perhaps inevitably, if they are more than fleeting) comprise multiple bonds. Our relationships with one another are woven of various human attachments—personal likings, common interests, shared work, family connections, friendships, and loyalties arising from shared history. All these will exist alongside the bonds of kinship in and through Christ. Some of the time, as his own life indicates, these may pull us in quite different directions.

Still, Bonhoeffer does not describe loving faithfully as a Christian as a matter of chopping away those other attachments, paring down our relationships with other human beings to the one, sole, objective, and completely "impersonal" fact of being joined by God's grace in Christ. Instead it consists in acting according to what he calls "the truth." It means that our loves must be governed by this realization: that this person whom we enjoy and delight in, long for, and (yes) desire as a companion or a partner or the child long awaited, is first and last and always the daughter or son of God. He or she is one redeemed by Christ and claimed by him for God's own, and this may sometimes mean that the one we love must be given up as a companion, "despite all the protests of [our] human love."

Examples of this are common in history as in the present. A letter written by Augustine, fourth-century North African bishop, responds to the reproaches of his dear friends that he is so far away and so occupied with the affairs of his office that they are always deprived of his company. He writes that often we learn our duties from the needs of those whom God entrusts to our care, and that the obligations of his calling transcend his own grief and even the grief of his closest friends.

There are many, many contemporary analogues to this—people who leave home and family for the sake of a call to duty, and families who must respond to such a call with encourage-ment and support, despite the painful personal cost. This is true for those called to religious service, but also for those who serve as diplomats abroad, as doctors in disaster areas, or in military service around the globe.

But it is not only special missions that may require sacrifice: the commitments of ordinary family life are also profound, and our loyalty to them may in fact require that we give up other relationships. It is not for nothing that marriage vows include the promise to "forsake all others."

I do not wish to minimize the seriousness of Bonhoeffer's demand that human loves and the enjoyments they seek might have to be forfeited if they conflict with our duties or our call-ing as Christians. Bonhoeffer does see human and Christian love as distinct and sometimes deeply at odds. But I do want to under-line that he expects pain and protest in such circumstances, and he does not indicate that this is anything to be ashamed of.

Human beings are in fact attached to one another. We do long for intimacy and we naturally want the companionship and physical presence of those we love. In the end, Bonhoeffer seems to suggest, Christians will not and need not suppress or annihi-late such human loves. They have rather to see that they may have to be surrendered for the sake of something even more funda-mental: the recognition that the one we love is who she or he is first in relation to God and not to us.

All this becomes more vivid and concrete if we return for a moment to the story of Bonhoeffer's life, sketched earlier. We know from his writing as well as from the testimony of close friends and relatives who survived the war that Dietrich was a man with many warm personal relationships. He had seven brothers and sisters, including a twin sister, Sabine, to whom he was especially close. We have some of his letters from prison and they reveal great concern and affection for his family and for the various friends who came, when they were allowed, bringing him books and comfort and small practical gifts. During his impris-onment, many of his friends and associates in the resistance were likewise in prison, undergoing interrogation and the threat of death. His anxieties for them could not be safely expressed. In addition, in January 1943, just three months before his arrest, Bonhoeffer had become engaged to be married.

His letters, which had to pass the scrutiny of Nazi censors, are restrained and careful. Still, they are alive with feeling, with personality and the sweet particular memories and concerns of friends and family members. The existence of such letters reminds us that Dietrich Bonhoeffer had real attachments in this world, people he worried over and longed for and grieved never to see. He had made choices all along that put those human relationships at risk, including returning to Germany from safety in the United States when the situation in his homeland was clearly deteriorating. He walked steadily toward the end he felt called to, to the particular shape his discipleship took. But he did not do it woodenly, without grief and longing, without sorrow and regret.

As the extent of his involvement in the plot against Hitler was uncovered over time and the likelihood of his execution became greater, he expressed concern lest his attachments to this life would cause him to behave other than honorably and courageously. However, he did not reproach himself for them. They were the shape of a human life in the world, and holiness had to be made out of them and with them, not over their graves.

LOVE, HUMAN AND DIVINE

Nygren and Bonhoeffer questioned whether our ordinary human attachments have anything much to do with the love of God and whether they are even compatible with the love that God commands. I have already given reasons for resisting at least some of their conclusions. Still, this conversation remains important, in part because it has helped to shape the last one hundred years of Christian thought about love. But it is also important because it challenges many of the things we tend to take for granted in our own time and place. If an earlier generation of Christians wondered whether our natural loves could be related to the love that God offers, we have the opposite problem: we have trouble seeing that there is any real difference between them. We fail to recognize any tension at all between what we might mean by love and what the biblical writers or the saints meant by it.

The signs of this assumption are all around us. As I write this, stores are setting up their Christmas displays and advertising campaigns. Bright placards and beautifully decorated windows invite us to "remember what the holiday is all about" by planning lavish meals and thoughtful gifts to bestow upon family and friends. Cards stacked in the aisles of my local drug store announce that "Christmas is love"; they're illustrated with plump, happy toddlers on Grandma's lap clutching teddy bears. Such sentiments and images are appealing.

But looking at these cards one would never suspect that the first Christmas took place in a stable or that the poor couple with their rather embarrassing pregnancy had no relatives with presents beside them. Certainly nothing in our cultural celebrations encourages us to remember how terribly costly the love brought to birth in the Nativity turned out to be, particularly for that vulnerable little family. (By contrast, an old tradition had Christians store their Christmas trees away in the attic to dry out through the winter. In the spring the branches would be cut away, leaving the trunk for the center piece of the cross displayed on Good Friday.)

Even in the Church we often assume that the love that binds the Christian community is no more than a modest expansion of our ordinary attachments to family and friends. We celebrate baptisms, and everyone shares the family's delight in their new baby. The confirmation class comes forward and we elbow each other to say, "Look how tall he's gotten!" or "What a young lady she's turning into!" We gather at weddings and listen to the reading of 1 Corinthians 13 about love being the greatest thing and never failing, and rarely does the preacher point out that Paul isn't talking here about romance but about patience and a love that "suffers long" (KJV).

There is, of course, nothing at all the matter with our enjoyment of babies, our pride in growing children, or the hope and excitement we all feel at weddings. To the extent that these things turn our attention beyond our immediate personal connections to the children and the marriages that belong to us simply because they are part of the larger body of the Church, they are all to the good. But in themselves they do not press us very far. If nothing else is done it is more likely that churchgoers will gradually enlarge their circle of personal attachments rather than form ideas about the Body of Christ. Even less likely is that they will conceive of a love that reaches even beyond that Body to the unknown, the unlikely, and the unresponsive.

There are two problems with this state of affairs. First, it doesn't prompt us even to *think* beyond our society's general expectations of polite indifference to strangers and restrained hostility toward enemies. It is easily compatible with a rather banal ethic of civic decency in which we take care of our own and don't actively harm anyone else (unless they harm us first!). But if that is all the gospel inspires, then Jesus' pointed question comes to mind: "What do you do more than the unbelievers?" (Matt. 5:47). It makes one wonder whether the things Christians believe make any difference in their lives. This is an issue considered at more length in later chapters.

The second problem is that the lack of more serious reflection about the character or the requirements of Christian love leaves us impoverished. It gives us no new resources for sustaining our day-to-day relationships with spouses and children, parents and siblings, coworkers and neighbors—relationships in which we often struggle. Human loves not anchored in the reality of Christ's redemptive love depend for their survival on their ability to give us what we want. When they do not, we easily abandon them or distort them beyond recognition.

In churches that do little to challenge or deepen our assumptions about love, perhaps it is not surprising that the rates of divorce, child abuse, and family problems related to drugs or alcohol are no lower among observant Christians, including morally conservative evangelicals, than they are in the population in general. It appears that even human loves as such cannot flourish without something like the self-giving love of God.

Whatever the centuries of Christian thought and practice regarding love might have to offer, it is of no practical help to us unless we first learn to pay attention to its fundamental claim: that the love of God made flesh in Jesus Christ reveals something new in the world, and in doing so makes possible—and necessary—a new and different way of life. In the next chapter we take up the question of what obstacles get in the way of human efforts to love, and how the things Christians believe and do together might help to address them.

3

Practicing (at) Love

Not very long ago I spent an intense and completely enjoyable evening with a friend. Four hours flew by without our noticing it as our conversation ranged over the usual topics shared between good friends: work, family, mutual acquaintances, projects, challenges each of us was facing, and so on. Partly because of the work we both do and partly because of the personal stories we had been exchanging, near the end of our time together my friend exclaimed, "Why are love relationships so *hard*?" Thinking about that question, through reading and in conversation with this friend and others, has been a significant part of provocation and preparation for this book.

Even smart, competent, and highly successful people—those who may be deservedly well-regarded in their professional lives, who have all the gifts of attractive personalities and are deeply committed to living kindly and responsibly in their relationships with others—find it hard to sustain loving relationships. Sometimes, despite all their serious efforts, their gifts, and their best intentions, relationships fail, ending with visible fractures or invisible walls, reduced to politeness or worse. Other times relationships are sustained but with deep and lasting wounds. These wounds not only inflict pain on the participants but also limit and distort their other relationships. If loving those near to us well is hard enough, it is no wonder a human love that extends to strangers and enemies is hard even to imagine.

Throughout the remainder of this book we will be seeking a middle way. We want to recognize all the dramatic differences

between God and human beings but still take seriously the biblical expectation that we respond to God's love in love for God
and each other. We want to be able to acknowledge that the
affection we have for those nearest to us is not in itself a complete response to, or a sufficient reflection of, the encompassing
love of God that reaches out to enemies. At the same time we
don't want to be forced to conclude that human and divine love
are unrelated, or even permanently hostile to each other.

For one thing, such a judgment seems to neglect too much
of scripture and Christian witness. It also ignores too much of our
experience of grace as well as challenge in human loves. More
than anything, we want to learn what Christian wisdom about
love can do to enrich and sustain our ordinary lives and loves, and
whether it can help us heal those that are damaged or broken.

Rather than starting with a general and abstract account of
Christian understandings about love, it may be more helpful to
begin at the other end. We will start with a closer look at our
experience of the things that limit and distort, hinder and undermine our efforts to give and receive love. Then we may be in a
better position to see how the convictions and practices of Christian life may help us learn to love better—more wisely, more
consistently, and with a wider embrace.

Eventually the love that Christian tradition talks about will
come to challenge our complete preoccupation with those nearest to us. But as our ancestors in the faith will show, the same
understanding and the same way of life that will turn us outward
to the world can enable us to love better close to home.

WHY IS LOVE SO HARD?

In a general way we have already considered some of the reasons
for our difficulties in the previous chapter. There we talked about
all the fundamental differences between human beings and God
that make it impossible for any human love to model God's love
fully. We are, as we noted, mortal, finite, morally inconsistent, and
dependent on things outside ourselves. We are also, as Christians
understand it, created, blessed, called, and redeemed by God, and

in these convictions lies the hope Christians have about the possibility of our coming to love well and faithfully.

Nonetheless, our limits and the challenges to love that arise out of them are real and we have to take them into account. It is important to take a sober look at how these features of human existence shape the character of our loves and how they can hinder our ability to love God and one another.

We start from the fact that we are *needy* and that from the beginning of our lives we turn to other people to have our needs met. This is of course just a fact about human beings, one built into us, so to speak. Human infants (unlike many other creatures) come into the world completely helpless and must rely on the constant care and protection of adult human beings if they are to survive infancy. They must be fed, kept warm and dry, and protected from all the risks in the environment to which they find their way if left unattended. In addition, children's period of dependence is prolonged, lasting more than a decade even in societies much simpler than our own. The relationship that develops with the person (or persons) who serve as protector of the child is the first and primary model for all relationships thereafter. (This is why people whose early caretakers were unreliable, cold, or even actively hostile so often have lifelong problems forming other human attachments.)

As we mature, of course, we become able to meet many of our needs ourselves. But because human beings are social animals, we continue to have basic and permanent needs for the company, approval, and affection of other people. All these features of human beings are givens: we cannot choose to be otherwise. From a Christian standpoint, these characteristics are also part of the created nature of human beings that God declares to be "very good." Our neediness cannot be disregarded, but neither should it be despised or denigrated. It is not corrupt in itself but is just an aspect of being the sort of creatures we are. However, under the conditions of distortion and alienation from God that Christians call *fallenness,* our neediness tends to be an occasion of corruption. Part of taking this aspect of human beings seriously is looking hard at the effects it may have on how we see the world and how we act within it.

Control Seeking

Because part of what we need is other people and because having basic needs go unmet is painful at best and terrifying at worst, it is always a temptation to ensure that our needs are met by controlling others. This can take a thousand different forms. Sometimes we seek control directly or even violently, as in political struggles, legal contests, or economic competition. In close personal relationships, the forms of control may be very subtle and perhaps not even fully recognized by the person using them. We manipulate other people's vulnerabilities, play on their emotions, and use fear or guilt or pity to extract the behavior we want from them. (Think of all the countless variations on "If you really loved me, you would. . . .")

This manipulation is often not calculated and it may not even be conscious, although sometimes we feel uncomfortable or uneasy about it. (Likewise, when we are on the receiving end we may feel vaguely angry or resentful and then may feel guilty about the resentment, making the manipulation all the more effective.) Even if we are unable to recognize or name exactly what is going on, the effects on our relationships are deadening. Spontaneity is replaced by a dull feeling of constraint and coercion, the joy of genuine human connection is dampened by unease and suspicion, and anxiety and a sense of falsity eat away at the real intimacy we desire. Our efforts to guarantee the outcome we want actually cost us something vital in the relationship.

Jealousy

The people on whom we depend are, like us, limited in their time, energy, and attention. This can cause us to feel insecure about getting what we need from those we love and make us resent the other people to whom our loved ones are connected. The classic example of this is the intense jealousy that very small children sometimes act out toward new siblings. This behavior is easy to understand in children, who are physically dependent on their parents' care and emotionally dependent on their attention and approval. (One psychologist notes how much trouble we would have persuading another adult with the kind of reassurance we often use to calm children in these circumstances. Imagine telling your spouse that you were enjoying your relationship with him or her so very much that you decided to bring home another husband or wife to make your family life even happier![1])

In fact, similar feelings (if not, usually, similar actions) are found among adults, even in relationships that are not exclusive. We want assurance that the people on whom we rely will be available to us when we need them, and we may also want to be the one on whom they in turn rely. We desire to please the people we love, but we also want to be important to them, maybe more important than others.

Most of the time we do our best to hide such reactions. But think of the last time a close friend of yours made a new friend and waxed enthusiastic about him or her in your presence. If there wasn't at least a twinge of resentment, of "pay attention to *me!*" you are unusually secure and generous.

Such feelings of possessiveness suggest that our focus in such a relationship is on how it nourishes us rather than solely on the good of our friend. (Otherwise we might be able to celebrate with our friend in the good fortune of finding a new friend to enrich his or her life.) Because jealousy (like manipulation) is extremely unattractive,[2] it can undermine relationships like romance and friendship that depend heavily on attraction and mutual enjoyment. So here is another instance when our very anxiety to ensure that our needs for affection and affirmation are met can have the opposite effect.

Loneliness

Also related to our neediness is the experience of loneliness. A sense of chilling isolation, that no one shares our joys or pains, that no one really understands or cares deeply for us, can come to us even in the presence of other people. It can coexist with all our busyness, even in a life crowded with relationships. As an old popular song has it, one can be alone in a crowded room. Probably everyone has had the experience at a party of feeling intensely a stranger in the midst of dozens of casual acquaintances, an experience only made more painful by the need to maintain the appearance of having a good time.

If we lack the sense of being known and attended to as the person we know ourselves to be, we can feel as if we have in some sense disappeared, ceased to be a person in ceasing to be known and cherished as one. This can feel like being deprived of the very air we breathe. Crucially, this experience depends less on what is true—whether we are in fact known and loved by other people—than on what we perceive. But what we perceive depends partly on other things: day-to-day events, physical health, fatigue, stress, and all of the many factors that influence our emotions. It is probable that all human beings feel lonely at least some of the time; in fact, it is often one of the shocks of early married life to discover that marriage does not mean one will never be lonely again.

Whether or not they realistically reflect our situation, even relatively brief periods of loneliness can be intensely painful. In the midst of such a powerful experience of emptiness, the desire for something (or someone) to fill the void within us is compelling. Sometimes loneliness serves to drive us out of ourselves, into new and rich connections with other human beings. The danger, however, is that we will settle for something less than such a real connection. We may not be seeking a relationship of genuine mutuality and respect; we may not be attending to the reality of the other person at all, but merely making him or her into a bandage for our own wounds, a plug to fill the void we feel inside. Without ever meaning to, it is possible to do grave harm to those whom we use to ease our loneliness or distract us from it. It is also possible to wrong deeply the people we overlook, the people in our lives whose love, for a time at least, fails to reach or comfort us.

Self-Deception

As deep in us as the need for the approval and regard of others is the need to maintain a view of ourselves we can respect and affirm. In fact, an important aspect of the affirmation we seek from other people is that it supports and confirms our belief in ourselves as worthwhile. The discussion of self-esteem has been carried to the point of comedy in certain quarters, particularly in relation to child-rearing, and it has left some parents afraid to criticize or correct their children no matter what their behavior. But such exaggeration should not hide the fact that we do need, and strive to maintain, a basic level of positive self-regard.

This is the most ordinary sort of observation: that we wish to think well of ourselves and that we resist and are pained by suggestions that we are less than admirable in some way. This is why criticism is unpleasant, no matter how well-intended or constructive, no matter how carefully expressed. An important part of coming to maturity is learning to accept and profit from criticism, but probably no one enjoys the experience. In one sense, criticism is harder to accept when we recognize its accuracy. This is because justified criticism forces us to see ourselves differently, to incorporate new and unwelcome information into our understanding of who and what we are.

What I have said so far applies in all kinds of relationships and settings, from educational contexts to work evaluations to the casual comments of acquaintances. But it has a particular force and represents a special challenge in close relationships, with the people who know us best and see us in all kinds of circumstances. These are the people who have the most grounds to criticize, the most information, and they are also likely to be the ones most hurt by our failures and our faults. At the same time, their criticism cuts most deeply. It is the most painful to hear and the hardest to come to terms with.

Of course these are also the people most involved in our lives and most likely to have a stake of their own in how they see us. They are perhaps, in being the closest, also the least objective observers, something we are likely to remind ourselves of if their criticisms seem harsh or one-sided. Both points are valid and it is not always easy to sort out truth from distortion. The day-to-day business of reckoning with the corrections or reproaches of those who matter most to us—deciding what to take at face value, what to reject, and how to respond—is a huge part of the texture of our personal lives.

But here we have uncovered both the gift and the great challenge of loving relationships, something of what makes them so *hard,* as my friend observed. Love is hard because on the one hand it *requires* real knowledge of human beings and on the other hand it *permits* such knowledge. And the truth about human beings is always a mixed and inconsistent thing. Sustaining loving relationships is difficult because they are hard on our illusions: our illusions about other people and, even more painfully, our illusions about ourselves. They force us to revise our self-understanding where it departs from the reality others see.

Real intimacy is costly because it involves penetrating some of our self-deception. The self-knowledge that comes to us in human relationships of genuine depth may be more than we want to know. It is not easy to build a foundation for self-esteem that can withstand unwelcome truths, even though they can open us up to new growth. Sometimes we prefer to cling to our illusions, even if it means giving up the intimacy we crave.

Fear

Linked to all these other patterns, perhaps even the common foundation that underlies all of them, is fear. We are deeply, viscerally aware of our neediness and of our dependence on other people to fulfill our needs and enable us to flourish. We know from experience that this is a risky business, that our need for connection to other human beings also opens us up to the possibility of being hurt or rejected, disappointed or abandoned. Because the human needs we seek to have met in loving relationships are so basic, we cannot give up the search for love or the effort to sustain it, but neither can we easily give up the effort to keep ourselves safe. We do this in a variety of ways, testing the depth and reliability of a relationship and trying to figure out how much weight it will bear and how much of ourselves we should entrust to it.

This dynamic is most obvious in romance, where both partners try to take careful (and matching) steps toward intimacy and commitment. Each is pulled in one direction by a desire not to lose the other's interest and in the other direction by the fear of moving too fast and risking too much. There is a similar delicacy in the early stages of a friendship as we negotiate the long path from mere acquaintance to trusted confidant. In all such contexts it is easy to see how fear of loss, humiliation, or betrayal keeps us from fully offering ourselves and from being fully willing to receive the other.

Some of this is ordinary prudence, the reasonable effort to move slowly into relationships where we make ourselves significantly vulnerable. But moving toward trust requires both discernment and a kind of courage, and there is no way forward that is free of risk. Insisting on certainty beforehand, choosing self-protection over relationship as a life pattern, amounts to the same thing as choosing isolation.

In one sense, this challenge never disappears. The risks of human relationship are hardly over once the walls have come down, once dating or acquaintance has progressed to committed relationship or serious friendship. Human beings continue to fail one another: they withhold what is needed, they are unable to see clearly or to love unselfishly, they lose hope and confidence and withdraw. New occasions for anxiety arise, new threats appear, and fear itself remains a significant barrier to human loves.

Fear keeps us from disclosing what is true, but also from seeing what is before us. Our vision is distorted by what we are afraid of: we see the threats more clearly than the possibilities, the risks we face rather than the risks we represent to others. This limits our ability to receive and to care for the people we might love. And if self-protectiveness is a factor in our approaches to romantic relationships and friendships, it is overwhelmingly the limiting factor in our response to strangers. Finally, mutual (and perhaps mutually well-founded) distrust is virtually the definition of what it means to have an enemy. It is also the most stubborn barrier to any possibility of reconciliation.

WHAT CAN HELP?

All of these patterns—control seeking, jealousy, loneliness, self-deception, and fear—arise out of the character of human beings as vulnerable and dependent for their flourishing on things outside themselves. They are the shadow side of our powerful impulses toward companionship and communion, and they represent our sometimes desperate efforts to obtain what we need in human relationships. The irony, of course, is that all these tendencies work as obstacles to our fulfillment, because they are barriers to genuine love. Just how contrary they are is clear when we consider the following description of love offered by theologian H. Richard Niebuhr, often quoted because it expresses something of what has proven difficult to pin down:

> Love is rejoicing over the existence of the beloved one; it is the desire that he be rather than not be; it is longing for his presence when he is absent; it is happiness in the thought of him; it is profound satisfaction over everything that makes him great and glorious. Love is gratitude; it is thankfulness for the existence of the beloved. . . . It is a gratitude that does not seek equality; it is wonder over the other's gift of himself in companionship. Love is reverence; it keeps its distance even as it draws near; it does not seek to absorb the other in the self nor want to be absorbed by it; it rejoices in the otherness of the other; it desires the beloved to be what he is and does not seek to refashion him into a replica of the self. . . . In all love there is an element of that holy fear which is not a form of flight but rather deep respect for the otherness of the beloved and the profound unwillingness to violate his integrity. Love is loyalty; it is the willingness to let the self be destroyed rather than that the beloved should cease to be.[3]

Rejoicing. Gratitude. Reverence. Respect. Loyalty. Such a picture is persuasive for what it captures of our deepest and most significant experiences of loving. These are the loves that light our lives, that order our daily routines and give meaning to our daily struggles. But this description also highlights the way in which all the needs or tendencies listed earlier in this chapter are at odds with our desire for love, even though they may be rooted in it.

The contrast is only made more extreme if we take up the hint offered in Niebuhr's last line and consider the New Testament's insistence on defining love in relation to the cross, as a complete and even reckless self-giving for the sake of the beloved. Such a profound investment in those we love could trump all our desires for safety and fulfillment. No wonder, then, that Christian thinkers have sometimes doubted that human beings have the capacity for the freedom and self-forgetfulness that genuine love requires.

But as we saw in the first chapter, the New Testament also suggests otherwise, in its commands and its exhortation, in its pastoral counsel, and even in the praises it sings to God. For over and over again it commands that we love: love God with our whole self and all its powers, and love one another not only as we love ourselves (which is often poorly enough!) but even as we have been loved by God. From Paul to the Gospels, from the letters of John to the letter to the Hebrews, the New Testament prays for and commends and rejoices in God's work of uniting us to God, to one another, and to the world for which Christ is offered.

The Bible tells us that love is the duty of Christian ministers, the responsibility of Christian spouses and parents, and the test and touchstone of all Christian conduct. But it also tells us that love is the gift of God, the work of the cross, and the fruit of the Holy Spirit. Because God has sent the Son, love is possible. Because Christ has come and died and risen, love can be known to us. Because the Spirit remains with us, love can be lived out among us. This is the very shape of redemption, that for which the church exclaims, "Glory and thanks be to God!"

This all may sound impossibly idealistic and remote, and the fact that the Bible commands something may seem a long way from showing that we can do it. But another look at where our struggles to love and be loved go wrong may show how Christian faith and above all Christian life as it is steadily practiced in a community might give us unexpected resources for healing and hope.

Worship Limits Control Seeking

If the first barrier to genuine love is a self-centered temptation to control others, the first and most fundamental confession that Christians make is that God is God. To call any being "God" is already to acknowledge that the world is governed, and by someone other than us. To name as God the One who is revealed in scripture—through creation and the saga of Israel and finally in the life, death, and resurrection of Jesus—is to confess that the world is ultimately ruled by wisdom, power, and self-giving love. This is to declare as a bedrock truth that the universe is not merely random, not simply a constellation of chances and threats through which we must each make our own way as well as we are able. Instead it is a creation made and beloved by God and destined for fulfillment.

At the same time, according to the story Christians tell, it is a world lost and in rebellion, where alienation from God runs through everything as a fatal flaw, like a crack through the heart of a diamond. It is never simply benign, and all its creatures are subject to both accident and evil. But because God has not abandoned the world but continues to call and direct it toward its true end, it is still possible to declare with prophets and psalmists and with generations of believers the world over that God reigns.

Making such an affirmation is more than just assenting to a proposition, like agreeing that the moon is made of rock rather than green cheese. The proclamation that God reigns calls forth and sustains certain attitudes toward human life, dispositions such as humility and confidence and trust in God. It also calls forth an acceptance of all that is beyond our control. This is an acceptance quite different from mere grim resignation. It is based on the belief that God's will is directed toward our good and that God's wisdom about the shape of that good is greater than our own and remains so even when it is deeply hidden from us.

The Christian practice that corresponds to naming God as God is worship. A central part of worship, a feature that runs through Christian liturgies from the East to the West, from high church to low, and from Catholic to Protestant to Orthodox is simply the declaration of God's sovereign greatness. In psalm and prayer and hymn,

Christians proclaim God's goodness and mercy over all God's works, God's might and majesty in ordering all according to God's wisdom. Christians are constrained by their diverse liturgies to declare continually that God and God alone is Lord.

By the practice of worship, Christians are schooled not merely to acknowledge that fact but also to welcome and celebrate it. Those who really are formed in these habits of mind and heart, who really have nourished the attitudes of humility, confidence, and trust that worship instills, have less reason than most people to cling to illusions of control over their own lives or over the lives of others. Their confession teaches them already that they cannot bend the world to their desires and that they cannot wrest what they need from others by force or manipulation. They remain vulnerable and dependent on the gifts of God and others—others who, like them, belong to God and answer ultimately only to God. God reigns, and that is good news.

The Eucharist Responds to Jealousy

While the limitations of human beings, their finite capacities for attention and energy and presence, give rise to jealousy, the infinite riches of God's love make all competition for divine favor absurd. God does not run out of time, is not too occupied with one petitioner to attend to another, does not expend too much compassion on one creature to spare any for another. Even to put it so sounds foolish. In fact, not only is our experience of the love of God not diluted by the communal character of the church's life, by the presence of others who are likewise loved by God, but it is enhanced and enriched by it.

How God is experienced and made known in the world is what theologians call the *divine economy* (from the Greek *oikonomia,* household order). But God's economy does not operate like our economies on a principle of scarcity, where everything valuable exists in limited amounts and has to be parceled out among competitors. Instead, it operates on the principle of abundance.[4]

The "one thing needful," as one Gospel puts it (Luke 10:42), the pearl of great price (Matt. 13:46), is simply the gift of God's saving mercy, the scope and depth and fullness of which cannot be plumbed, much less exhausted. To share God's love is not to lessen it but to increase it, even to increase one's own experience of it, for by loving we begin to enter into God's own life in the world.

The practice that most fully embodies this experience of God as the One whose love nourishes and sustains all who come, without limit or loss, is the Eucharist. Called by different names and marked by many rituals across the wide range of Christian traditions, its common elements make it instantly recognizable in all its forms. Here Christians gather to present themselves for healing and renewal, to be pardoned by the One who knows all and still welcomes, to be fed and strengthened for the journey. Here they come, in whatever state they can manage, to the table that Christ sets for them. They can be confident of being received, for at this meal he is both Host and Bread, and the food is as inexhaustible as God's own mercy.

Those who are formed by this steady practice have a kind of bulwark against the desperation that can make us grasp after one another or drive away those who threaten our share of love and attention. They need never be absolutely hungry, and they know that love, at least, does not always have to be parceled out, measured, and hoarded lest we go away empty. Christians do not, of course, lose their need for other human beings or for the embodied forms of human love. But they eat regularly at the Table where all are fed, and there they are nourished by a love that grows rather than being diminished in the sharing.

Prayer Answers Loneliness

Although it sometimes seems that a great fear of aloneness must underlie much of our frantic social activity, Christians know that they are never entirely alone. They can never be apart from God, not even in those times of fear or challenge when they might prefer to escape God's continual and daunting presence. (Anyone who has ever sought to escape an uneasy conscience can appreciate the ambivalence of the psalmist who cries, "Whither shall I flee from your presence? . . . If I ascend to heaven, Thou art there! If I make my bed in Sheol, Thou art there!" (Ps. 139:7–8).

According to the understanding of God shared by Christians and Jews, God does not simply exist in the world, like a really big item in the inventory of the universe. Instead, the world may be said to exist in God: not as a part of God, but rather as a reality held in being and sustained by God's reality. Likewise, God is not inside of time and space but rather time and space are in a certain sense inside of God; they are creatures in the same way that material things are creatures, and their existence depends on God. There is nowhere and no "when" in which God is not first and always already there.

The practice that enacts this awareness of God's continual immediacy is prayer. Of all the practices of Christian life, this one may be the most difficult to explain to someone who has no real experience with it. The simple definition that we give to children—that prayer is talking to God—may in fact be as good as any. Still, it can be no better than a pale metaphor, and of course there may be no speech at all in prayer. Prayer is essentially conversational, but it is a conversation that is not really bound by words, even when words are its medium.

You will come a little nearer the idea if you think of talking with your best and oldest friend, the one to whom you do not ever have to explain things, who knows what you are not saying and what you are afraid to say, and who is there waiting for you when you find the words. In prayer we are in a communion like no other, perfectly revealed by God's knowledge and perfectly secure in God's love. There is a sweetness to this, the one relationship in which nothing can ever be or need ever be held back, an absolute intimacy that cannot be described, and it is at every moment nearer than your next breath. For this reason, the presence of God is the most complete and reliable answer to the terror of loneliness, because God's knowledge and understanding are absolute and God's love is unshakable and unmixed.

All this Christians affirm with confidence, but here it is necessary to acknowledge something that may seem to undermine everything I have just said. As I observed earlier, loneliness depends less on the truth about whether we are known and embraced than on whether we experience ourselves as so embraced, understood and cherished by some other person. The fact that God's constant presence and love can be affirmed does not always mean that they can be experienced by a particular human being at a given time, even when they are sought in earnest. The same book of psalms that proclaims (or complains of) God's inescapable presence also laments and protests God's felt absence, the seeming abandonment that makes the writers cry out that God has forsaken them.

But in fact the inclusion of such declarations in the Psalter already suggests the answer of faith—that confidence is expressed even in the outcry itself, for it is always to God that the cries are addressed. The despair of psalmists and prophets is not fully black, for it is expressed within the framework of a relationship. It is for this reason that even the psalms of lament so often end with the proclamation of God's saving mercy. The experience of loneliness and the apparent withdrawal of God occur within a long history that is still trusted, even when all that can be seen is darkness and all that can be heard is the silence of God.

Confession Corrects Self-Deception

Although human beings almost reflexively avoid having to recognize or admit their faults in their relationships with one another, a relationship with God creates a space in which self-disclosure is safe and concealment is futile. What's more, the central claim of Christian faith, that we have a Savior, depends on the prior assumption that we are, all of us, in need of one. Because the "good news" the church announces is nothing other than the forgiveness of sins made available in Christ, the acknowledgment of one's need is the universal and sole entry requirement.

The kind of self-knowledge offered and required within the Christian community can be painful enough and is a self-insight into which a person grows over time. (It is a common observation that it is not those newest in their faith who have the keenest sense of personal sin but those of longest standing, even though their behavior may appear far better to an observer.) But the pain of coming to see oneself more truthfully is framed within the experience of grace—the forgiving and transforming grace of God, and the embodied grace of a community that welcomes sinners not with judgment or disdain but with recognition: "Here is one of us."

In line with this fundamental understanding, Christians make a regular and public habit of announcing their sins, or at least the fact of them, out loud. Of course these public prayers of confession vary widely in their character as well as their form, and some may be so generic and toothless that they barely recall our real sins to our minds. They may also at times sound more like a description of accidental errors and well-intentioned misunderstandings than actual confessions of willful and responsible wrongdoing. But with all their limitations, they nevertheless school believers in the habit of self-accusation rather than self-justification.

Because so many of our offenses against God take the form of failures in fairness, honesty, patience, and kindness toward other people, we can hardly enter into the task of self-examination without confronting all the issues of our relationships. Confession offers a constant reminder that we hurt others as often as we are hurt, and that we disappoint as often as we are disappointed by those we love. Most important, the practices of confession and pardon instill by repetition a basic lesson: that our connections to God and one another rest not on success but on mercy, and that forgiveness is the ordinary texture of a shared life. The charity on which we all depend "keeps no record of wrongs," we are taught (1 Cor. 13:5 NIV). We don't have to get it right, which means we don't have to pretend to have done so, and some of our dearly held illusions about ourselves can be allowed to fall.

Consecration Answers Fear

Earlier I suggested that fear might be the underlying commonality underneath all the barriers to love we've identified. If that is right, it may help explain why the words "Do not be afraid!"

show up so often in the Bible. More familiar as the "Fear not!" of the King James Version, these are often the first words out of the mouths of the various angels who appear as messengers, and they are the reliable accompaniment to every powerful manifestation of God. The words *do not fear* are the climax of every prophetic declaration that God will save God's people, and they are repeated by Jesus over and over: to the disciples on the stormy lake, to those seeking healing, in his final speech before ascending to heaven, and on many other occasions.

It is hard to understand how this offer of comfort that is also a command makes sense, and how we might be expected to follow it. It would be easier if we could take these words as simple reassurance, a promise that nothing bad will happen, the way we might mean them if we said them to a small child on the first day of kindergarten. In fact, it is common enough, even in churches, to hear people talk as if Christians can and should count on divine protection from danger and disaster. But it is hard to interpret "do not be afraid" in quite that way when it occurs in scripture. After all, some of the biblical "reassurance" sounds pretty extraordinary:

> Beware of them, for they will deliver you to councils, and flog you. . . . And you will be dragged before governors and kings for my sake. . . . Brother will betray brother to death, and the father his child, and children will rise against parents, and have them put to death. . . . If they have called the master of the house Beelzebub, how much more will they malign those of his household! Therefore have no fear of them. [Matt. 10:17–18, 21, 25–26)

"*Therefore* have no fear of them"? In the middle of this talk of floggings and death? One feels there must be a step missing, somehow. But of course the passage goes on to offer an explanation— of sorts:

> Do not fear those who kill the body but cannot kill the soul; rather fear him who can destroy both soul and body in hell.

Are not two sparrows sold for a penny? But not one of them can fall to the ground without your Father's will. Even the hairs of your head are numbered; fear not, therefore; you are of more value than many sparrows. [Matt. 10:28–31]

Those women and men across the centuries who have found their sustenance here have found its comfort to be profound. But it will not do to gloss over the strange character of that comfort. It does not rest on the promise that all will go well, that we will be preserved from peril and pain. In fact, as we have seen, it does not even seem to promise survival. Rather, it promises that God's will is our security and that God is our final home and our ultimate protection.

Such confidence is available only to those who have learned over a long, slow growth of years to entrust themselves completely to God, those who offer themselves, their lives, and all they have and all they love to God to be used according to God's good pleasure. They find in God's faithfulness the one true safety, which nothing can threaten, and the satisfaction they look for is deeply anchored in the love of God itself. It is that communion toward which they look with longing and hope. But such a confidence depends ultimately on a horizon that stretches out beyond history, to a fulfillment and a vindication that no one living can see. Only those who can place their trust there, in God's unshakeable purpose of redemption, can say with Martin Luther, "You cannot harm me, for I am baptized."[5]

The practice that corresponds to the finding of safety in God alone is the one Christians call *consecration*. It is an aspect of many events in the life and liturgy of the Church, from the baptism or dedication of infants to the ordaining of ministers to the prayers offered for the sick and dying. In all these events as well as in the daily "your will be done" of the Lord's Prayer, Christians practice this fundamental act, this finding of their identity and safety in God and God's will. And it is possible to see how this fundamental security might make it possible to take risks, including all the risks involved in daring to love and be loved by the fragile and unreliable beings we humans turn out to be.

If human love sometimes seems like walking a tightrope, then the practices of faith remind us that there is a net. But just as love takes practice, so does faith. It takes practice, a whole life's worth of practice, to come even haltingly to be able to repeat with confidence the words of the psalmist: "God is our refuge and strength, a very present help in trouble . . . therefore we will not fear, though the earth change" (Ps. 46:2).

PRACTICING (AT) FAITH

This chapter is a simple sketch of the central practices of Christian life and how they might nurture and heal our ability to love wisely and faithfully. The trouble is, in trying to be brief, any such sketch can hardly help making it sound much more pat and simple than it ever is or can be. So here it is important to say outright all the things that aren't true.

It is not true that a person who engages in these activities, and even one who sincerely believes the affirmations on which they rest, is thereby once and for all set free from all the things that bind us. It is perfectly possible (and indeed perfectly ordinary) to rise from your knees in worship and immediately set out to take control of your own life and the lives of all those who impinge upon it. It is likewise easy and commonplace to continue to experience and act out jealousy and loneliness, to turn willfully from the truths others would show us about ourselves, and to live in fear that drives us to distort or abandon our relationships with others. Faith offers us another way to live; it does not mean we will always follow it—it is a long, slow path toward healing and not an instant cure.

It is also not true that faith will solve all your problems. Christian faith is a form of life, not a magic answer. It offers confidence in God, not a panacea—not a promise of safety or painlessness or success. This is not "five weeks to a perfect life." The confessions of Christian faith—that God reigns, that God's abundance is unfailing, that God is continuously present, that God's mercy is endless, that God's salvation is secure—these convictions form the ground under our feet. The practices of Christian faith are simply how one learns to walk on this ground, how one learns to walk more nearly in love. It is the work of a lifetime, and there is no promise that the journey will always be easy.

Finally, we have in this chapter discussed human love as if it were one kind of thing, one way of responding to another being, when our experience tells us that we mean many different things by love. Although central aspects of love—such as the gratitude and loyalty Niebuhr names earlier—may be common to all love's varieties, still we know that the character of our feelings for an old and trusted friend are quite different from those we have toward a romantic partner, and both are distinct from the feelings (just as deep and passionate) that bind us to our children.

The shape that love takes when these relationships are thriving depends not only on the person we love but also on the nature of the relationship. (In fact, one sign that things have gone awry is that the kind of love felt or the means of its expression does not fit the relationship; think of the spouse who wants to govern and protect the partner as though the partner were a child, or conversely the child who is treated like a buddy by a parent unwilling to assume parental authority.) As our loves are different, so are the ways in which they may be illuminated by Christian convictions and sustained by Christian practices. Now it is time to speak more particularly of the different loves that animate our lives and make them rich—and often difficult. What inspires these various loves and what is the nature of their fulfillment? On the other side, what is likely to go wrong with them and how can we understand and respond to the problems that arise in them?

The Variety of Loves

On a recent visit to the house I grew up in, I was rummaging in the back of the spice cabinet looking for something and came upon a small glass jar. It was perhaps four inches tall, with a faded blue and white label. The label marked the jar with brand and contents, but I didn't need to read it. I had seen this thing at intervals my whole life and I knew it contained a mixture of cinnamon and sugar. We had used it to sprinkle on toast and oatmeal and sliced apples throughout my childhood. I cannot imagine how many times this jar with its perforated top must have been refilled over the decades, and I can't remember a time when it wasn't there in the cabinet, waiting. The only surprising thing about this perfectly pedestrian object was the pleasure I felt when I saw it. It brought an instant rush of what could only be called affection, the peculiar power that attaches us to what is simply familiar, and for no other reason. What I thought to myself was, "I love this little jar!"

This homely example, so far down the scale of what we mean by love, nevertheless highlights something obvious in our common experience. This is that the things we call "love," while they have a certain unity, are at the same time strikingly diverse. Up to this point we have treated love as if it were all one thing: one constellation of feelings, attitudes, and motives, one more or less uniform core of positive appreciation or desire. But a moment's reflection or an hour's attention to how we talk immediately shows that to be far from accurate.

To take only a small step up from our attachment to familiar objects, we routinely say that we love cheesecake or hyacinths or fresh-fallen snow. We may mean by this something quite superficial: simply that we enjoy the taste or smell or sight of these things. To call this "love" rather than (as an earlier generation of grammar teachers would have insisted) "liking" might be just exaggeration. But we might also mean something rather profound. The qualities—the richness or the sweetness or the stillness—of these particular things may stand for a whole realm of goodness in the world, forms of loveliness for which our delight and gratitude may be deep and important. Perhaps, then, the word *love* is not entirely out of place.

Similarly, we might say we love Shakespeare or Bach or Rodin and mean just that we enjoy their work, a response that is a mixture of aesthetic pleasure and intellectual appreciation. But we might also mean something much larger: a response to beauty itself, a sense of the depth and possibilities of human existence that the works of art call forth and that deserves to be called spiritual. Here too, to call this response love may not be far off.

We also commonly speak of love for animals, and this may be experienced as a deeply personal form of love, even if the animals cannot respond with the same sort of awareness. How powerful such attachments can be was illustrated in the aftermath of Hurricane Katrina, when some victims refused to be brought to safety if they could not bring their pets. They remained behind at their own peril rather than abandon the creatures who had been their companions; some of those who stayed were never rescued. To some people such an action seems silly, while to others it appears as understandable even if tragic.

Even when we confine our discussion of love to our love for other people, the word encompasses an enormous range of feelings, impulses, and kinds of connection. This is, of course, hardly a new observation. In the classical Greek discussions of love that form much of the background to Western thought, different words are used to distinguish between these different forms of love. Four of these words have become part of the vocabulary in modern reflections on the topic. We have encountered two of them already, in theologians' discussions of *eros* and *agape*—the loves of desire and of charity. To these can be added *storge* and *philia*.

Storge is the Greek word for affection, the basic, almost instinctive love for those closest to us. The fundamental instance of *storge* is our attachment to our parents, children, and other family members, the people who surround us and make up the first and primary relationships of our lives. In fact, familiarity is the only essential element in affection, and it is possible to feel it for those with whom one has very little in common beyond the ground of shared experience. Even liking is not strictly necessary: it is possible to be deeply attached to those who are not especially pleasant but who have always been around.

A very different kind of attachment is called *philia*. This is the love of friendship, which in the classical understanding is a relationship born of particular choice and intention. Here mutual appeal, not the mere accident of daily proximity, underlies the connection. The particular character and personality of the friend is all-important. Although we may make the acquaintance of a friend by happenstance, it is not happenstance that turns acquaintance into friendship. That depends on the development of the approval and admiration and mutual enjoyment that are an intrinsic part of what we mean by friendship. Other aspects of friendship—intimacy and trust and loyalty—grow up over time, but the soil out of which the relationship grows is a kind of attraction to the particular person as such.

If we are going to be able to use all the resources of Christian wisdom about love to illuminate our lives and nourish our relationships, we will want to probe much more deeply into the particularity that gives those relationships their character. We mean quite different things by these loves, and different things inspire and sustain them; accordingly, different things go wrong in them too. Using the time-honored categories of affection and friendship, romantic love, and the other-centered love of charity as a starting point, we can begin to explore all the rich variety that the language of love encompasses.

AFFECTION

Affection, the least exalted version of love, is the one we most take for granted and most rarely reflect on. But as the foundation of our attachments within families, affection is arguably the most pervasive and the most socially essential kind of bond between human beings. This is the love that unites us to the people with whom we share our daily lives, the love that ensures that the dinner gets made and the kids get looked after and the paycheck gets brought home. Out of affection we accomplish most of the ordinary stuff that makes life together possible.

The experience of affection is one of warmth, security, and at-home-ness. It is a kind of low-level background hum of well-being associated with things being "normal." Often the very mundane and virtually automatic character of the ties of affection makes them seem routine and unworthy of serious attention. When affection is present and operating, as within families, for example, or between longtime associates, we are inclined to take it as simply "natural," a matter of habit, almost, and not especially interesting. There is a reason that there are no great operas celebrating affection: it is such an ordinary, thoroughly domesticated kind of love.

How powerful and essential these bonds are becomes clear only when they are disrupted or when for some reason they fail to form. The loss of a relationship that is a primary bond of affection is at least acutely painful and may be devastating. The lack of ties of affection with other human beings is a developmental disaster for a child, and their complete absence in an adult is a sign of the severest kind of pathology.

The matter-of-fact or "accidental" character of affection does not mean it lacks intensity or particularity. Think, for example, of the deep and passionate attachment of parents to their children. That bond is the standard example of affection and remains among our most fundamental personal commitments—perhaps the deepest and most enduring attachment of which humans are capable. Losing a child is one of the most severe emotional traumas a person can endure. No one with any sense would try to comfort a parent who has suffered such a loss with the suggestion that he or she simply adopt a replacement.

Yet it is one of the characteristics of affection that it can grow to embrace those who would not otherwise be found attractive or enjoyable. We recognize this in the case of parent-child attachments in phrases like "a face only a mother could love," but under the irony is something profound. We are right to be moved by parents' capacity to be devoted to a child who is not attractive or rewarding, who may in fact be unable to respond at all, or who may respond in ways that cause only grief. There are other, more modest examples as well. Affection can and does spring up all over the place, uniting the most unlikely partners. It is the most democratic of loves.

To be the object of affection does not require that we be remarkable in any way, nor are we especially conscious of the attachment. Out of everyday experience grows expectation, habit, security, and a sense of well-being. We often become aware that affection has developed only after the fact. We notice it when the absence or the eventual return of someone we are used to having around affects our sense of things being "right." We find ourselves wondering with real concern, "Where is John from the mailroom? What happened to Mr. Kim who is always at the deli?" If they do not return, we may experience a genuine sense of personal loss.

The practical basis of affection is clear and obvious when the person in question meets some need, as when small children become deeply attached to their caretakers. But it springs up even where the person is simply part of the landscape of one's life, and daily contact alone may be the soil in which it grows. It may not even require liking, although affection may help us to notice what is likeable in another person.

In its power to unite those who are unlike us, who are not drawn together by attraction or desire or common interest, affection mirrors one aspect of the love of God. Its capacity to grow almost anywhere, with nearly anyone, offers a kind of finite and human-scaled image of the universal reach of God's love. At the same time, affection is as specific as any other love. It may grow up anywhere, but it loves the particular person, with all his or her features or even faults. One would not really want the grouchy but ever-present crossing guard to be replaced with a courteous stranger, or even to have the old guard back with a different personality. This too is an apt reflection of divine charity. If we believe that God loves us, that love must be extended to the particular persons we are—even when it is easy to imagine a new and improved version.

These, then, are the peculiar gifts and graces of affection: ordinariness and durability, expansiveness, and the ability to bind together those who have no basis for connection other than a shared life. But the rooting of affection in our connections with those who are nearest to us also makes it prone to particular limitations and distortions, and to things that weaken it or turn it aside. And like all human loves, it is vulnerable to corruption.

The most obvious and innocent limitation of affection is its dependence on familiarity. If it is natural enough to love those to whom we are most accustomed, it may be equally natural to ignore or even withdraw from those with whom one is not familiar. Unfamiliarity makes us uncomfortable, unsure of what to expect, anxious or ill at ease. The flip side of attachment to what is familiar is detachment from what is not.

The easy enjoyment of affection within one's regular circle means that welcoming the stranger takes a decided effort, an effort that affection itself will not prompt. The family and other such havens of affection may become a little like exclusive clubs, places that turn their members' attention and energy inward rather than outward. A family delighting in being reunited at home may think to invite the lonely new neighbor to join their Thanksgiving table, but affection will not move them to do so.

Familiarity also breeds complacency. We may come to take for granted people who are close to us in a way that is unjust and may even be fatal to their love, and ours. We may not attend to the love of our daily companions as a gift worthy of attention, gratitude, and appreciation. Given enough time, that absence of attention may cause affection on both sides to wither into pure routine, evacuated of meaning, or into a chill and joyless familial duty.

At the same time, the routine and reliable character of affection may also tempt us to think of it as *simply* automatic. Because it ordinarily takes so little to kindle affection between those who share their lives, it is easy to assume that one is somehow entitled to it and can claim it as a matter of right. "Of course you love me—I'm your father/mother/brother/sister/Great Aunt Agnes." Those who come to think this way will not often question what they have done to inspire affection, or ask what they might have done to extinguish it.

In reality, affection *can* fail to develop in situations where it is expected or even counted on, and it can die where it has once existed. Not only obvious mistreatment chokes it off. It can also be throttled by indifference, by thoughtlessly cruel criticism, or just by overwhelming self-preoccupation. Examples of the failure of affection are common, its residues only a kind of distance and the sense of lost possibility. When that happens, it is common to think of it with resignation, as "just one of those things." You will not find in popular magazines a dozen articles giving emergency advice about how to recapture closeness to a distant sibling. In fact, insight into how affection fails or goes wrong can be hard to come by.

Because the needs met by affection are so basic and so primary, and because we expect it as part of family life, we are often unreflective and uncritical about its inner workings. This lack of thoughtfulness makes it especially prone to all the destructive impulses we discussed in Chapter Three. Anxiety and possessiveness can distort and overwhelm any love, including affection. Those who find affection lacking where it is expected (even where this may be through their own fault) often grow resentful and self-absorbed. They are full of a sense of grievance.

Feeling continually hungry, such people are likely to cling and cloy and demand assurances of love and devotion, signs of an affection that cannot be summoned even by those who know they "ought" to feel it. Here we stumble upon one of the ironies of human love: that people who are desperate for reassurances of being loved become more and more difficult to love. Like gratitude, affection cannot be insisted on without being destroyed; the sparks that might kindle it are only trampled into lifelessness by insistence.

Still, the basic human needs that affection fills cannot readily be denied. At worst, when its corruption is nearly complete, what goes by the name of love may end up being reduced to pure hunger. This can take the form of a hunger to be looked after, as when a person continually demands to be nurtured and petted and reassured. It can also take an opposite form, a hunger to be important, to be necessary, to be *needed*. In the end, either of these may be corrupted altogether, turned into a willingness to devour another to fulfill one's own need or to cripple the ones we say we love in order that their need for us may never disappear.

Examples of both versions of this are easy to come by, in history as well as in contemporary life. The poet Elizabeth Barrett Browning, famous for her *Sonnets from the Portuguese,* was a captive daughter. She was the oldest of eleven children, and after her mother's death she remained virtually housebound, confined by poor health and by the refusal of her overbearing father to permit her to marry, until she was nearly forty. Robert Browning, who had begun a relationship with her by correspondence, finally persuaded her to elope with him secretly and launch a life of her own. We know from her letters that her sense of guilt over this was intense: her father refused ever to see or speak to her again.

Here is an example of the opposite corruption: I have known for thirty years a man now approaching fifty who lives at home with his aged (and exceptionally long-lived) parents. He has never moved out of the house, never gone beyond high school, never held a job, never had a romantic relationship—in short, never begun an adult life. In his case, it is not that his parents claim to need him but rather that he needs them. They instilled in him as a child and adolescent such an extreme timidity that he cannot face independent life. Doubtless all such parents would claim to love their children. Perhaps they even believe that they do.

FRIENDSHIP

When we in the modern world call someone a friend, we often use the word casually, to cover everything from the acquaintance we see from time to time at the kids' soccer matches to our dearest and most trusted confidant. Our casualness reflects the fact that we don't take friendship very seriously, either as a dimension of adult human life or as a subject for reflection—certainly not in comparison with people in earlier times. It is not uncommon for people to go for years after high school or college without forming a new relationship of any depth that is not romantic or familial. In our later grown-up lives, many of us no longer invest significant time in any relationship outside of those with romantic partners or our immediate family members.[1]

This state of affairs is due in part to a number of practical factors, such as the relatively transient nature of our communities and the increasing number of hours adults devote to juggling jobs and housework, child care and errands. There is also, however, the fact that friendship as a primary arena of human intimacy and personal growth has been replaced by an ideal of the spouse or partner as "best friend" and by the expectation that family relationships would provide all the companionship and support a person needs. For many adults, friendship has taken a back seat to romantic love and family life, coming in at best a distant third in an emotional landscape already compressed by the ever-growing demands on our time.

It is not surprising that it is the love of friendship that has suffered the greatest loss in our hurried and overscheduled lives. If affection is essential as the glue that holds families and societies together, friendship is at the opposite end of the spectrum of human loves. It is not socially necessary in the way that affection is, or even in the way that sexual and romantic love are necessary to the procreation and rearing of children. Friendship, as moral theologian Gilbert Meilaender has observed, is not needed for human survival, but merely for human flourishing.[2]

In saying so, Meilaender sides with an ancient tradition of philosophy and Christian thought that held that friendship is essential to a good and fully human life, and even to moral and spiritual growth. In his treatise on ethics, Aristotle devoted three whole books to the topic of friendship, because it is a central part of human well-being as he conceived it. By contrast, a contemporary treatise on moral philosophy would be unusual if it addressed the topic at all. Even to understand such a belief we have to explore what this tradition meant by the love we call friendship.

In the tradition coming down out of Plato and Aristotle, friendship means loving a good person for the sake of his or her goodness. True friendship, they taught, is based on virtue, on the excellences of character the friend possesses that attract others who have or aspire to those same qualities. Approval and admiration inspire friendship. Friendship was thus considered a particular type of love for the good as it is embodied in another person.

Of course these philosophers recognized that people can be good in different ways and that different people might prize and be attracted to those qualities to different degrees. They also had categories for other less significant and lasting kinds of friendship, those formed around mutual benefit or around some shared pleasure. (Here we might think of what we today call business associates or professional mentors or members of a sports team on which we play.)

But although these friendships of pleasure or utility might grow into something more over time, in themselves they are limited and passing. They depend on something valued outside the friend, and they fail when that good runs out. Business relationships come and go, professional mentors are eventually outgrown, and teams change or disband. It is in *virtue friendship,* as these philosophers called it, that the friend is loved for his or her own self. Here people are united in a lasting bond that shapes them, helping to form who and what they might become.[3]

We might expect friendships based on prizing good qualities of character to be detached, chilly, or purely intellectual—like a perpetual self-improvement regimen. Nothing could be further from the truth. In fact, the language of friendship in antiquity often seems odd to us now because it was so passionate. It was common for separated friends to write of their longing to see one another and to express their attachment in words we are likely to reserve for romantic loves. They often spoke of themselves as "halves of one whole" or as "one soul in two bodies."

These ancient writers express their keen enjoyment in the physical presence of the friend, the beloved face and voice, and the turns of phrase or ready wit as among the delights of friendship. Friendships were expected to grow and mature over years and to require a significant investment of time. Aristotle says that friends have to have eaten the required weight of salt together, a way of speaking of the countless meals shared by friends who take part in one another's daily lives.

In the ancient Greek and Roman worlds, friendships entailed loyalty, steadiness in difficulties, and a readiness to give help when it was needed. They were a support in adversity, a school for virtue, and a source of delight at all times. Friendship was regarded as a form of love central to a good and fulfilled life, and the very highest of human relationships.

This classical background became the basis for a specifically Christian understanding of friendship in which the virtue that unites Christian friends is the shared love of God; they are engaged in the common pursuit of holiness.[4] But such friendships do not merely express and celebrate Christian character: they also form it. Friendships have the power to clarify our vision of the good and to inspire and invigorate us in its pursuit. Spiritual friendships, as these relationships were called by early Christians, have been lifted up as an important means of growing in the knowledge and love of God, and of achieving holiness of life.

Still, it is not merely that spiritual friends seek holiness together, but that holiness is loved and prized as it appears in *this* particular friend, in the ways it is reflected in him or her. Specific persons bring out the best that is in *us,* kindle in *us* a longing for the goodness we glimpse together; these are the spiritual friends God has given to us.

One of the most famous examples of spiritual friendship is that between St. Francis of Assisi and St. Clare. Francis had helped Clare escape her disapproving family (through a hole made in the wall of her house) when as a seventeen-year-old girl she wished to enter the convent and embrace a life of poverty. They met only a few times for conversation and prayer, admonishing and encouraging each other in their pursuit of a purer and freer devotion to God. Later Clare formed an order of Franciscan nuns, the Poor Clares, which still exists today. Near the end of his life, when he was in anguish of body and spirit, Francis made a final visit to Clare at her convent. G. K. Chesterton relates a story told of them:

> One night the people of Assisi thought the trees and the holy house were on fire, and rushed up to extinguish the confla-gration. But they found all quiet within, where St. Francis broke bread with St. Clare at one of their rare meetings, and talked of the love of God. It would be hard to find a more perfect image for some sort of utterly pure and disembodied passion than that red halo round the two unconscious figures on the hill: a flame feeding on nothing and setting the very air on fire.[5]

Descriptions like these at least make it clear that what I mean by friendship depends on more than casual association and is more than the affection awakened by shared experience and shared activities. Even such companionship can go a long way toward easing a sense of isolation, and friendship may grow out of it. But the sense of being profoundly understood and prized for who one is, and of holding a common vision of what is true and important—all those things that make for a life richly and deeply shared—depends on forging a connection with another person who sees the world as we see it. This sense of friendship as join-ing in a kind of adventure, of supporting and also sometimes recalling one another to the pursuit of a vision, is unique and comparatively rare.

For this reason alone, as well as because of the investment of time and attention required for companionship to grow into friendship, this love is at the far end of the spectrum from affection in a second respect as well. It is not merely that the functioning of society does not depend on friendship, but that it cuts across all the bonds that hold our societies together. It unites particular people in a way that is selective and in a sense exclusive.

This does not mean that friendship depends on shutting others out intentionally. Such behavior would be the sign of a pseudofriendship, one in which internal bonds are missing and so must be replaced by the false unity of "us and not them." We see an example of this in the constantly shifting alliances of those, both children and adults, who must prove they are popular by associating with the right people and especially by excluding the less favored. In fact, true friendships are enriched by the introduction of more friends into the circle, as we enjoy the gifts that one friend brings out in another.

To maintain the character of friendship, however, friends must all be united by a degree of common understanding, by a view of life that enables them to delight together in something outside the relationship itself. This means that not every person can be loved as a friend, and what we call finding a friend is more like receiving a gift than like making a decision. All this may make friendship sound quite exalted, above the neediness of mere affection and the famous complications of romantic love. In fact, as the love of friendship is different from other loves, so are its challenges and its distortions—but challenges and distortions there certainly are. Some have been hinted at already. Friendship is selective by its nature. Where it can be extended it offers unique gifts, but human beings do not see one another or the world in such a way as to make universal friendship possible.

Friends can also develop a sort of shared arrogance that the relationship may serve to reinforce rather than challenge. Because friends share a kind of vision of what is important, it is not hard for them to come to feel superior to those who do not see what they see. This is true not only of those friendships formed around sweeping and comprehensive goods such as the pursuit of wisdom or the love of God. A shared sense of superiority can be seen as well in two friends who share a conviction that physics is "really" the fundamental science or that baseball is the purest form of sport.

This sense of "us against the world" is often enough harmless, even endearing. Family members may view with affection and indulgence (and a corresponding sense of superiority) the friend who "is always off in the corner with Dad looking at those silly butterflies" or engaged in some such pursuit. But sometimes, hardly realizing it, friends turn from prizing one another to dismissing outsiders. Their indifference to others' opinions about their shared passion subtly shifts from disinterest to real disdain.

Most important, the power of friendship can confirm our vision of the good and strengthen our commitment to it, and that is the case whether the commitment is wise or foolish, or even whether it is good or evil. The fact that friends share and confirm our vision of what is important helps to maintain the commitment and to insulate it from other judgments. This can fuel and sustain conspiracies to defraud or destroy as well as plans to reform or create. It is not by happenstance that close-knit groups of friends are likely to be found at the genesis of revolutions, not only the ones history comes to judge as good and necessary, but also those it comes to call *coups d'etat* and marks as catastrophes.

Even in the realm of spiritual vision, the power of friendship is not immune from corruptions that may be disastrous. It is not easy to distinguish from within between friends bound together in pursuit of an ideal and the devotees of a cult suffering under a kind of group delusion. If the Gospel of John indicates that the group of those who began as Jesus' disciples finished by being called his "friends" (15:15), it is also likely that the suicide cult gathered around Jim Jones at Jonestown and those who planned (and died in) the attacks of September 11 had once been friends.[6] Perhaps they would have said they were right up to the end.

ROMANTIC LOVE

By romantic love I mean something that creates a profound attachment, a capacity for deep commitment and significant sacrifice. Certainly it includes sexual attraction and desire as intrinsic parts. In fact, if desire were to be stripped away, what would remain would no longer properly be called romantic love. But this kind of love is not simply to be equated with a desire for sexual union, however intense that desire might be.

Instead, in romantic love sexual desire is taken up into an even more fundamental longing: the desire for a full and lasting personal union. This may be expressed and partly embodied in the sexual union, but it is hardly exhausted by it. The lover is capable of being entranced by the sight or sound of the beloved, delighted in his or her mere presence, filled almost to bursting with the excitement of being together, even if the immediate possibility of sexual intimacy is wholly foreclosed.

This is particularly the case in the early stages of a romantic attachment, the state we call "falling in love." Often, especially if the person in love is not already sexually experienced, the frankly sexual element may not be the first or dominant aspect of romantic love. It wells up later and may be experienced as almost beside the point, like thirst is beside the point for the lover of fine wine.

The romantic lover is taken up in admiration and fascination and wonder. The first sense is joy that such a creature as the beloved should exist. If the romantic passion and delight are returned, the sense of amazement and gratitude is itself compelling, almost intoxicating. In this state, not only the vision of the beloved but also the lover's whole experience is transformed. There is the sense that with the beloved you find your true self, or even that the two of you together constitute a whole world. Thus it is perfectly easy to be delighted with folding socks at the laundromat if you get to do it with your beloved, or even to hope that she or he will come by. This capacity to infuse the ordinary with mystery and excitement is one of the gifts of romantic love, part of its power and joy.

But of course romantic love does include sexual passion as part of its essence. Some of the intensity of romance comes from its being suffused with a longing for physical union that is part of a more comprehensive longing to receive wholly and be given wholly to the beloved. This too can be transformative, changing in a basic way the experience of being alive in a body and the relationship between body and self. In the popular movie *Shake-speare in Love,* the heroine rises from her first night in her lover's arms to answer the tentative call of her nurse, "It is a new day." She responds emphatically, "It is a new *world.*" All those who can recall their first experience of a genuine and full-blown sexual love know what she means.

In our cultural context, it hardly needs to be said that sex can be and often is another matter altogether, a simple, straightfor-ward, and direct pursuit of physical pleasure and release sought for its own sake. It may be emotionally neutral, separated from any kind of personal attachment; it may even serve to express hatred or contempt. It is often somewhere in the middle, a ten-tative groping toward a relationship of greater human depth. Finally, sex may also be entirely in service of something else: a means of making a living or purchasing favors or merely dis-tracting oneself from a loneliness that sex itself cannot remedy.

As unions of body and mind and emotion, we human beings, alone among the animals, invest our behavior with mean-ing. We have considerable choice about what meaning we give to it. It is not necessary that sex be the body's share in a complete and profound personal union; it is only possible. But it is worth noting that even in a cultural setting like ours, where sex with-out strings is relatively easy to come by, most people seem per-sistently to look for something more—something deeper and more compelling, even though it is also more elusive, more demanding, and more risky by far. Something in us reaches for a union that is not merely bodily but also fully personal and seems to find in it a taste of home—even a taste of heaven.

It is not hard to describe romantic love well enough to prompt recognition or to distinguish it from mere sexual desire. But it turns out to be very hard to explain what is at work in evoking in us this most intense, consuming, and exclusive of loves. It is not for want of trying. Poets and novelists, playwrights and lyricists, and (more recently) biologists, psychologists, and sociologists have expended enormous amounts of effort and ink in speculation and analysis.

Poets have written for millennia about beauty as the well-spring of romantic passion and about the lover's fulfillment of ideals of male or female perfection. Novelists have depicted the perceived qualities of mind or heart or spirit that are what we "fall in love" with, or the complexities of the personal dynamics that burst forth into romantic love. Scientists have contributed the thesis that we are attracted to mates whose offspring are like-liest to thrive, and psychologists have helped us sort out the models and images, good and bad, that we carry forward from our individual pasts and look for in (or project upon) our part-ners. Some of the literary treatments are moving and eloquent, and some of the insights of the natural and social sciences are illu-minating. None is fully convincing, for we have too much expe-rience of romantic loves that seem to defy all their explanations.

If you ask people why they love their partners, or try to think about what has prompted your own most serious roman-tic attachments, you are likely to come to a sort of impasse. It is easy enough to name things you love in a romantic partner, but after a while it is equally easy to name things you don't. And it is not at all clear whether you love the partner because she or he has these qualities or, rather, that you love the quali-ties partly because they are found in your partner. It is the par-ticularity of the person that one loves, not just the constellation of characteristics.

I recall a student in a class on the ethics of personal relation-ships who had just read a theory about romantic love being based on the partner's fulfillment of a gender ideal. A middle-aged woman married for twenty-five years, she carefully and thought-fully composed a list of the characteristics that were associated in her mind with the ideal man. To her chagrin, her husband of a quarter century possessed almost none of these qualities. Natu-rally it did not matter at all.

No one who is presently in love will be engaged in an ongo-ing assessment of whether the attractive qualities that could be named in the beloved might be more fully realized in some other person. (Indeed, the perception that a romantic partner is "shop-ping" in this way can prompt jealousy and a sense of betrayal quite as intense as that provoked by a particular other man or woman.)

Much of our language, including the phrase "falling in love," conveys the sense of romantic love as something that befalls one, for good or ill. Although this can be used as a kind of blank check to excuse all kinds of irresponsible behavior, it nevertheless reflects something that corresponds to our experience. Romantic love, even more than other forms of human love, is awakened, not decided on, and it is not simply a matter of will. When it happens, it feels like magic; perhaps this is why there is so much likening of romance to a spell under which one falls.

But there is an unhappy corollary. If we cannot exactly tell what makes us fall in love, there is a great deal of human experience to indicate that we also cannot directly understand or control what causes us to fall out of it—what makes romantic love wither and die. Famously, however, it can and all too often does die. Half the world's literature, it seems (and most of its country music), is devoted to lament or protest of that fact.

But here we come to a great contradiction: romantic love, particularly in its first rush, always feels absolute. It is always ready to lay claim to being eternal, proof against every challenge, immune to time and age and even death itself. It is famously characteristic of lovers to expect of themselves and one another eternal passion and eternal delight-in-loving. In fact, lovers are eager to promise these before any witness, human or divine, who can be made to listen. Music and poetry, both pedestrian and soaring, are full of such declarations.

And while romantic passion lasts, it is ready for any sacrifice and indeed makes all the hardest deeds of love easy, even effortless. It is a genuine pleasure to serve the beloved, and more rather than less so when the love is securely returned and no acts are needed to prompt a response. The lover looks for ways to delight and the hope of pleasing is motivation enough. For a while, at least, we get a taste of love as a kind of second nature, and it may seem that all the capacities for attention, patience, sensitivity, and unselfishness for which we labor in other contexts have been given to us in a moment. It is a joy to love and all barriers are swept away. It is generally not hard to get those in love to take vows. However, it may be very hard to get them—or even oneself—to keep them.

This is because romantic love depends on a kind of vision of the beloved, one that sees in him or her that which is prized and admired, delighted in and desired. But the vision can fail. It can fail because the beloved changes or because the lover does. Sometimes it fails because the vision was never true; he or she was not truly who we thought, or who we loved.

But it can also fail because we lose something of our ability to see what is really there. We can lose sight, or lose heart, or even simply forget to look.[7] Romantic love, for all its incomparable exaltation, remains fragile. It seems that one cannot realistically promise to be "in love" forever. The problems this raises in our society for the practice of marriage as a permanent union confront us at every turn. (We will return to these problems and to what might be done in the face of them in a later chapter.)

The reality, however, is not merely that romantic love can die despite its protestations of eternal fidelity. Under many circumstances, when it does die it leaves behind a well of grief, disappointment, and rage that may give rise to something very like hatred. From the point of view of the lover who loves no longer, the sight of the one who was once loved cannot fail to call forth grief and loss and guilt. From the standpoint of the one left behind, the one-time lover is the source of the most intense pain, feelings of rejection and worthlessness and betrayal that in turn often generate anger.

This is true even when the loss of love is gradual and from within—when it dies, one might say, a natural death. In cases where romantic love is the casualty of some new erotic attraction, the situation is even more emotionally volatile and explosive. The clichés of melodrama about the violence and desperation of jilted lovers have a source in real life. Regardless of what sacrifice might be willingly undertaken in the name of romantic passion, that passion seems unable to tolerate the sacrifice of the relationship itself. The beloved may have anything at all—except the liberty to withdraw love.[8]

LOVE OF NEIGHBOR

Now, finally, we return to the love called in Greek *agape,* the love at the center of Christian life. It is most often translated by Christian thinkers as "love of neighbor" because of the New Testament's repeated command to "love your neighbor as yourself." But of course neighbor love applies to more than those who are near to us in one way or another. It names the love that is to be offered to all persons just because they are persons, and it explicitly includes strangers and even enemies. It is the form of human love that most directly and fully imitates the love of God.

This discussion is brief, but not because this kind of love is not important; Christians are in fact committed to the belief that this is the ultimate form of love of which we are capable and in some sense a touchstone for all the others. The discussion is brief because this love is seen in human life mostly in glimpses. It appears in flashes of compassion and sympathy for strangers, in acts of mercy and self-giving for which there is no obvious basis and no return. It takes us beyond the "business as usual" of our other loves, with their limitations and their general expectations of reciprocity, into love for love's own sake. Indeed, it is tempting to think of this love as completely beyond us, and many have argued that what appears as love of neighbor is really some other form of love or even some form of self-interest in disguise. But there is powerful evidence to the contrary.

Periodically some disaster moves hundreds or thousands of people to put their own lives and projects on hold. They travel at considerable trouble and expense to help efforts at rescue or reconstruction on the other side of the continent or the other side of the globe—efforts that will benefit no one they know or would otherwise ever see.

As I write this, hundreds of volunteers ranging from college students to retirees remain at work along the Gulf Coast of the United States, helping with clearing and reconstruction of the areas damaged by Hurricane Katrina in August 2005. Thousands more volunteers are scattered across the huge swath of Southeast Asia still devastated by the record-breaking tsunami at the end of 2004.

Today, one week after the event, volunteers from all over the world remain at work in the Philippines. They join survivors and military personnel in digging by hand through a hundred feet of mud, trying to free those believed to be trapped in a school by the catastrophic mudslide that buried a whole village. They continue even though they have been warned that the mud remains unstable and could shift and bury them in turn. It is hard to understand such behavior as anything other than an expression of love for perfect strangers.

The human love of neighbor is seen less often but most strikingly in acts of kindness offered to enemies, and even of this most difficult form of love there are stunning examples. Several years ago a Baptist minister in southeast Washington, D.C., lost his teenage son to a drive-by shooting. As does not often happen in this city, this boy's killer was apprehended and convicted—and sent to the prison where the minister worked in prison ministry. Not only did the minister bring himself to visit and shepherd this lost young man, but when the prison term was ended, the minister brought him into his own home, offering him the kind of fathering the young man had never received. Thus was ended a long cycle of misery and rage and violence.[9] It may be that claims that such love is impossible or illusory serve only to let us off the hook for this most challenging form of love, the furthest reach of human capacities for goodness.

There is no doubt that love of neighbor is challenging. It is a sort of love for which only the barest beginnings are given in human nature and experience. Unlike affection, friendship, and romantic love, which grow partly out of our needs, our attraction to goodness, and our desires, love of neighbor has no built-in foundation beyond our capacity to recognize another human being as somehow like us and to empathize with him or her. (It is for this reason that the first three loves are called *natural loves,* while charity or neighbor love is understood in Christian tradition as God's work in us.)

Out of this basic capacity for identification with another person must develop a concern for the other as him- or herself, for his or her own sake. For our actions to be shaped by love of neighbor requires that we lay aside our preoccupation with ourselves and practice a kind of self-forgetfulness that human beings rarely achieve and even more rarely sustain.

According to Christian teaching, the process by which love of neighbor grows in us is both begun and continued by God. In the language of Thomas Aquinas, twelfth-century mystic and philosopher of the medieval Catholic Church, love of neighbor is a *supernatural virtue,* something that must come to us from outside the boundaries of human existence. It is not, like prudence or justice, simply the product of a good upbringing or a sound moral education or of life lived in a well-ordered society. It comes as the gift of grace.

As we saw in 1 John, such love is begun in us by being received. "We love because [Christ] first loved us": loved us although there was no natural attractiveness to draw him, no common cause to attach him, no need of his that we might fill or good we might offer. In him, God who is complete in all ways and can need nothing at all from us nevertheless comes to us for our sake. It is in our response to this divine self-gift that we see and delight in, and so are drawn to and begin to imitate, a love that is pure gift.

It is not true, on the other hand, that only Christians, or even only believers in God, can act out of love of neighbor. All human beings receive the gifts of God's grace, whether these are recognized as such or not, and all have at least the potential for responding. But the life of Christian faith is understood to serve as the training ground for love of neighbor.

The ongoing life of the believer is one of continual dependence on God's gifts, continual reliance on mercy, continual feeding at the Eucharistic table. It is therefore a constant practice in receiving more than one "deserves." This practice is what makes Christian life a constant and constantly renewed formation in the life of love, as God's own love is shared with us in word and sacrament and in the body of the Church, which receives and cares for us. The human response of imitation, the longing to "love as God loves," is at the heart of all Christian understandings of holiness. It is those who show the marks of this gift having been cultivated and taken root, who are filled with God's love not merely in flashes but as a pattern of life, whom we call *saints.*

Because love of neighbor is by definition modeled on God's universal and generous self-giving, we cannot really speak of its limitations or corruptions. But it is easy to think of things that have been claimed as Christian love of neighbor that reveal themselves to be otherwise. Sometimes this is a matter of transparent deception. In the European colonial era, for example, concern for the souls of the "heathen" was offered as an excuse for acts of the sheerest exploitation and domination across the globe, including the practice of slavery. More commonly, the free and self-giving love of neighbor becomes intertwined with other motives, both good and bad, sometimes consciously and other times in ways that are hidden from us. At such times the acts of love we undertake may be overcome or compromised by needs or desires or illusions that turn them into something rather different.

Black civil rights leaders in the 1960s were confronted by busloads of white liberal college students who came to join in the fight for voting rights and an end to legal segregation. They came to help, and they made significant sacrifices and took significant risks to do so. In a few cases they even lost their lives. But they came for other reasons, too, and brought other motivations with them. Even with all good intentions, some of them were unable to be of much help because they were not prepared to fill a supporting role. After all, they had come from some of the most elite academic institutions in the country, and everything in their backgrounds had prepared them for leadership. They had come to the rescue, as they believed; without very much thought they rather expected to be in charge.[10] This attitude can be attributed more to immaturity than to any settled conviction of their own superiority. It serves only as an example of how subtly even our best impulses can become tinged with less admirable motivations.

THE MUDDLED REALITY

Having spent all this time sorting out all the different things we call love, it is now important to acknowledge what a moment's reflection will make obvious: none of these loves exists for very long in human life in isolation from the others. Because we are and will always remain mixed in our nature, compounded of power and weakness, of gift and need, so our human loves are always made up of complex and various motives and feelings. In them, delight and desire, need and generosity, wonder and familiarity succeed each other by turns, even moment by moment.

This means that in our relationships, the various kinds of love are always commingled. Familial affection reaches over into friendship, as we age and come to have genuine admiration for the people who just happen to have been our parents. If we are lucky, our children grow into adults we can appreciate and admire, and they can appreciate and admire us, and the long and joyful work of parenting culminates in a kind of friendship.

Likewise, over time those who are united as friends develop affection for the other's incidental characteristics. They come to enjoy (or even to be attached to without enjoying) any number of features in each other that were not part of what originally drew them together in mutual appreciation. Similarly, lovers do not merely long for union with one another in a continuous ecstatic passion; they also (if they are fortunate) become friends. One of the great gifts of contemporary expectations of basic equality in marriage is that it makes friendship between the partners more likely and more complete. Alternatively, lovers may begin as friends so that it is the love of friendship onto which romance is grafted. When this happens, the friendship is transformed but not left behind.

And in romantic relationships, as is inevitable in any human relationship extended through time, the power of familiarity is also at work. No marriage, no matter how enduring and passionate the romantic love that began it, continues long without the aspect of (as the song has it) growing "accustomed to your face." The dailiness of married life ensures that affection infuses its routines, as shared time and shared tasks add the undramatic but real pleasure of partnership to romantic passion and friendship. Those who lose their marriage partners to death or even those who lose them to divorce report with surprise how much the sudden loss of the other's simply familiar presence adds to their grief.

This overlapping of affection, friendship, and romantic passion also applies to those relationships that begin as enactments of neighbor love. It does not take very many nights of serving at the soup kitchen or providing respite care for the elderly or child care at the women's shelter to find oneself bound by ties of familiarity and affection to those one serves and to those with whom the service is offered. Such settings are sometimes the birthplace of unique and important friendships, or even powerful romantic attachments. As a seminary professor I have attended many weddings of couples who met in some form of ministry.

But the movement is also in the other direction. Regardless of how much one may love a child, a friend, or a spouse, and no matter how strong are the bonds of affection and friendship or how strong is the vital attraction and delight that may endure throughout the years of a good marriage, there will still be times when these loves seem temporarily to desert us. At least there are times when these loves alone are not enough to draw from us the deeds that love demands.

On a particular day, the elderly aunt's anxious fretting is just one more demand to be quieted, the child's whining makes you want to scream, the friend is in need of support and attention you don't have time to give, and the spouse seems self-absorbed and unreasonable. At such times (and they are perennial) it is the restraint, the patience, the forgiveness of charity that fill the gaps left by the variations in our natural loves.

This is not to say that love of neighbor can replace or permanently substitute for the other forms of love. Certainly one would have to have an extraordinary degree of Christian charity to sustain the continuing demands of family life or friendship or marriage in their absence. Even if it could be done, the loss would be genuine and devastating. It is rather that the practiced love of neighbor can offer support when our other loves falter or lose their way. In those in whom it is well developed, love of neighbor may be able to offer sustenance through more extended periods of dryness or darkness, when the pleasure of caring for family and friends is gone or the vision of the partner that inspires romantic love is obscured.

Love of neighbor does not only enable us to do what is needed for someone even when we do not feel like it (although this is vital to sustaining a marriage or a family). It also enables us to pay attention to the other, making possible a renewal of vision and hope when those things that evoke our natural loves seem for a time to go cold. It is possible, sustained by charity, to give ourselves time and opportunity to fall in love all over again.

5

The Problem
of Self-Love

We have been trying to understand why the loves that bind us to others are often so hard: hard to nurture, hard to sustain, hard to find peace in. We talked in general about how fear and our sense of vulnerability make our loves fragile and liable to distortion. We also looked more closely at the different kinds of love we experience, seeking the particular ways in which they can falter or fail or go wrong altogether and become self-consuming. All these failures have one thing in common: in one way or another they involve a shift in focus away from the one we set out to love back to ourselves and our own needs.

This "turn to the self" is not always obvious, and it does not always look like what we usually think of as selfish. Our needs may well include things that are natural or even seemingly admirable: the need to be needed, the need to be loved in return, even the need to come to the rescue. An experienced pastor friend of mine talks ruefully about ministers with a "Mighty Mouse" theology, after the 1950s cartoon hero whose cry was, "Here I come, to save the day!" Unfortunately, in the long run this approach may have more benefit for the rescuer (who gets to be important and powerful) than for those who are supposedly helped.

Psychologists talk about relationships that get frozen into this pattern, where one person counts on being saved and the other person counts just as much on doing the saving. Both are trapped in a mutually reinforcing exchange called codependency, which can even squelch movements toward greater health. I watched this in action when my oldest friend, the child of two alcoholics and herself an active alcoholic from the age of fifteen, finally began the long journey toward recovery.

Nearly twenty years of drinking had brought her close to death and she began to attend Alcoholics Anonymous meetings in a last bid for survival. It was a slow and painful road that involved coming to terms with both the suffering she had endured as a child and the suffering she had inflicted as an adult on those who loved her. But the most difficult passage came after she had achieved a few years of sobriety, when she began to emerge from the fog of alcohol and renew her gifts as a creative artist and designer.

She was experiencing new professional success and personal affirmation, deeply rewarded by the role she was able to play in supporting the recovery of other alcoholics. And then, stunningly, her endlessly patient husband—the one who had supported her while she was incapacitated, who had carried her in off the lawn drunk and unconscious, who had cleaned up after her vomiting and made excuses when she didn't show up for work—left her. He no longer felt needed, and frankly he did not know what to do with the strong and talented woman who had appeared in place of the charismatic cripple he had married. His years of devoted service were revealed as really a kind of self-service. He needed her illness and could not bear to give it up, not even to save her life.

Whether in obvious forms or ones as hidden as this, the common thread of focus on our own needs raises again the question of whether human loves are really only a disguised form of self-concern. Can creatures such as we are *ever* learn to love well: freely, faithfully, generously? Or are we, as some theologians have maintained, completely captive to self-interest so that our human loves must be overcome and replaced by divine love that merely runs *through* us, like water through a pipe? If we are going to take such questions seriously, we will need to think again about the pervasive assumption of our culture that love for ourselves is at least innocent, if not a positive duty.

THE PURSUIT OF HAPPINESS

There may be nothing more characteristic of our age than its direct and cheerful affirmation of love for oneself. Advice to "be good to yourself," "take care of yourself," even to "indulge yourself" shouts from the covers of books and the placards on buses. The importance of loving yourself is touted by talk show hosts, celebrities, and public experts of all sorts. Much of this, of course, is merely advertising and its purpose is frankly commercial. Our self-care is expected to involve buying something, from the latest in hair coloring to that weekend getaway in the Bahamas, from exercise equipment to (paradoxically) the world's richest chocolate fudge cake. But some of it is more serious.

One source of this affirmation is the prominence of psychotherapeutic language within American culture. Along with offering private consultation, therapists anchor TV shows, host radio call-in hours, and write columns in magazines and newspapers. ("Dr. Phil"—clinical psychologist Philip McGraw—is a well-known example.) Much of their advice is put forward as guidance in the pursuit of fulfillment and personal flourishing. Because in our society the individual is thought of as the center of experience, meaning, and value, it is not surprising that the understanding of flourishing (at least as it comes through in pop culture) is most often individual as well.

Even when the topic is relationships, the aim of therapy is to be sure that these relationships meet the *individual's* needs, that they offer his or her best path to happiness and self-realization. For those who cannot afford a therapist, or who prefer to seek their emotional well-being on their own, there are countless resources for self-help. A stroll through the aisles of your local bookstore will reveal couples' manuals with titles like *Getting the Love You Want,*[1] and even spiritual guidance comes in books with titles that promise *Your Best Life Now.*[2]

All of this is easy to parody,[3] but the consequences of such a narrow focus on individual satisfaction are quite serious. For example, a number of recent studies document the damaging fallout of the dramatic rise in the rate of divorce over the last forty years,[4] a trend partly driven by the conviction that a marriage that does not bring personal happiness to an individual ought to be abandoned. But even apart from the moral questions that might be raised about it, there seems to be something going wrong with our pursuit of self-fulfillment.

In the last few decades, various experts have compiled a great deal of evidence to show that, on average, we Americans are actually doing a pretty poor job of taking care of ourselves on any number of fronts. We work longer hours than previous generations, both inside and outside the home. We take less time for leisure and even for sleep. We eat badly, consuming too much food of poor nutritional value, and we exercise little or not at all. We remain for decades in jobs and patterns of life that we report as stressful and deeply unsatisfying, and show the effects in rising rates of stress-related illnesses, both physical and emotional.

We are also more socially isolated, devoting less time to significant relationships with either family or friends. For all the emphasis on finding personally rewarding romantic relationships, not only do our first marriages end in divorce in record proportions, but these are followed by second or third marriages whose failure rates are even higher. If as a society we are more focused than ever on loving ourselves, there is much to suggest that we are not very good at it.[5] No wonder the market for self-help books is booming!

So what is the answer? Is it that we abandon our quest for individual fulfillment and instead find meaning in committing ourselves to broader social goals or simply in meeting our responsibilities to others? Is it that we continue to focus on our own well-being and just figure out better ways to balance career advancement, self-care, and social stimulation? Both of these and many suggestions in between have been offered by a range of pastors, moralists, social commentators, and mental health experts.

Underneath these questions is another, more fundamental question still: How should we love ourselves? Is there a right and proper self-love, one that really does lead us toward our flourishing? Could such a love of self be compatible with our loves for those near to us, or even with a kind of love that reaches out to embrace all people? Or is all this talk of loving oneself just evidence of the victory of self-indulgence in modern culture, an abandonment of our long-held moral ideals of duty and sacrifice?

SELF-LOVE IN CHRISTIAN TRADITION

The contributions of Christian thought to this debate can be found, confusingly enough, on both sides. On one side, particularly in its Protestant branches, Christian traditions include deep suspicion of any talk of love for the self. This is based in part on biblical depictions of the Christian life as one of self-denial, requiring that we "deny ourselves, and take up our crosses, and follow" Christ (Mark 8:34). This strand of teaching takes as its watchword, "Anyone who does not hate . . . even his own life cannot be my disciple" (Luke 14:26). This body of Christian reflection views pride as the central human sin from which all others flow, and pride is understood to include both overreaching in relation to God and preoccupation with the self and its interests. Such self-preoccupation is the very mark of fallen humanity, something to be resisted and overcome.

Accordingly, this strand of Christian thought interprets the repeated biblical command to "love God . . . and your neighbor as yourself" to mean that love of the self should be rigorously suppressed in favor of the love of God and neighbor. The injunction to love "as you love yourself" means not that we ought to love ourselves but that we should use our concern for ourselves as the measure by which we judge what we owe to others. In turn, the proper love of neighbor is understood in terms of selflessness: the other is to be loved with no regard or concern for the self at all. This is the interpretation given to Paul's statement, "Love seeks not its own" (1 Cor. 13:5, KJV). The moral ideal toward which this understanding points is self-sacrifice.

This was the position taken by reformer Martin Luther. He wrote about the love for neighbors that animates Christian life as "entirely free," completely indifferent to any human response or return. It is "pure love," as he called it, "love for nothing."[6]

Luther's ideas have been developed with even more force and consistency by thinkers like those we considered in Chapter Two. For all these theologians, self-love is the fatal infection of fallen humanity, the fruit of pride and the very heart of human rebellion and sin. In this view there can be no such thing as proper love for the self.

Even the Fourth century North African bishop Augustine, who has been accused by some of Luther's heirs of tolerating far too much self-concern within the confines of Christian life, was keenly aware and profoundly critical of human selfishness. He found evidence of human fallenness already in the behavior of infants at the breast, as they greedily suckle and protest having to share their milk with others.[7] His diagnosis of the condition that binds human beings and keeps them from right relation with God and with all creation is a kind of obsessive self-concern. Centuries later, Luther coined a phrase to capture this view: human beings are born "curved in upon themselves," and so turned away from God, who alone can satisfy.

But here already the other side of Christian reflection on self-love comes into view. It is true that Augustine and others like him use "loving the self at the expense of God"[8] as the definition of those who belong to the Earthly City, as the mark of all that stands in rebellion and under the judgment of God. This description is contrasted with "loving God at the expense of the self,"[9] which is the charter of the City of God that will endure into eternity. So far this sounds very much like the "denial of self" language just cited. But Augustine also writes of God as the one Absolute Good which fills and overwhelms the human heart, quieting all its desires and giving it true and lasting joy.

Augustine stresses that the longing for God is part of what God has built into human beings, and we are created to find our fulfillment only in God. To love God first is therefore both our duty and our delight. He concludes, "You have made us for Yourself, O Lord, and our hearts are restless until they find their rest in You."[10] The ultimate moral ideal to which theologians like Augustine point is not really the suppression of self-love in favor of love for others. It is instead a vision of love rightly ordered, with the love of God being both the source and the limit of all proper loves for created things. Only those who love God above all else can love God's creatures, including themselves, as they should. But those who do know and love God *will* love every creature for the real goodness it has, for God has made it and declared it good.

Augustine's spiritual autobiography, the *Confessions,* is written as an extended prayer. In it he expresses his gratitude for the gift of faith that has brought him to the peace of communion with God, whom he calls "my late-found Joy."[11] When Augustine writes of his own long wandering in sensuality and false philosophies, he sometimes accuses himself of loving himself or his friends too much. He says he loved in a fashion out of keeping with the true nature of those whom he loved, which was finite and mortal, captive to sin, and in desperate need of God. But in other passages he accuses himself instead of self-hatred and calls his intense devotion to his friends "friendship all unfriendly,"[12] because he used his influence over them to draw them further away from God. By contrast, he argues, true love for himself and for his friends would have required that he love God first and best.

Both ways of speaking make sense, and both echo scripture. The language of self-denial, of "hating" or "losing" your life in order to save it, is present in the Gospels (Matt. 10:37, Luke 14:26). But the idea that trust in and devotion toward God are at the same time the only path to human flourishing and so the only real way to love oneself is also deeply woven through the Bible and the whole of Christian thought. We find it in the plea to Israel in Deuteronomy 30:19 to "choose life!" by abiding by the Covenant given to Moses, and in the advice of sages in Proverbs to seek Wisdom and follow the commandments, "for length of days and abundant welfare they will give you" (Prov. 3:2).

The idea that true self-love requires faithfulness to God is found in the New Testament as well. In Luke's parable (12:18–21), the newly wealthy man who puts his trust in full storehouses instead of sharing his wealth with the poor is called not wicked but *foolish,* because he has placed his confidence in what cannot save him.[13] Even Jesus' command to sell all and give it to the poor has this promise attached: "And you will have treasure in heaven" (Mark 10:21). Somehow the love to which we are called is also ultimately connected with our own deepest well-being. Jesus says that he has come in order that we might have life in abundance (John 10:10). Those who lose their life for the sake of the gospel really *will* find it.

So it is possible for Christians sometimes to speak of the love of self as the enemy of the right love of God and neighbor, and at other times to treat self-love as a natural and proper part of that love, something truly found only in relation to it. Much depends, of course, on what we mean by self-love. Which way of speaking is fitting, which will point in the right direction, depends to some extent on the particular person being addressed. But it also depends on the context in which the guidance will be heard. When our culture bombards us with messages that we should love ourselves, we have good reason to ask about the motive behind those messages and about whether the version of self-love they promote is believable. In the end, how we think about self-love will depend on what we think human beings are and what we think a rich and fulfilling life would look like.

One of the saddest conversations I have ever had was with a man in his fifties who had just survived a massive heart attack. To tell the truth, this was a man I had never liked at all. I had gone to see him only because he was an old friend of my parents; they were out of the country and could not come themselves, so they asked me to visit him. I went and sat by his bed, prepared to make polite inquiries, to offer my parents' concern and best wishes, and to be out of there in fifteen minutes. (I know how callous that sounds. It was: it is not much of an excuse to say that I was only eighteen at the time.)

What really happened is that I listened for more than an hour, trying to think of something comforting to say while this man talked about what was suddenly, pressingly, on his mind. He told me that realizing he might have died, that he might still die, had shown him something terrible. Even though he had achieved what he had set out to do in his life, had everything he used to think he wanted, he now saw it wasn't worth anything. He had a pretty wife and a beautiful home and a white-collar job and a daughter and a son and a cat and a parakeet—but none of them liked each other very much. Come to think of it, he didn't like any of them very much either. The sad thing was, he didn't really have any better idea of how to go about making a satisfying life other than by gathering up the things he wanted. I had nothing much of any help to say to him back then, but at least I left the room liking him a lot better than when I'd come in.

As we turn to consider the complicated relationship between our love for ourselves and our love for God and other people, it will help to keep the mixed testimony of Christian tradition in mind. How is it that self-love can operate sometimes to limit and undermine our loves for God and other people, and at other times to call them forth and nourish them? Perhaps the best way to get some insight into this question is to begin with how we first learn to love and at the way human loves are bound up with our vulnerability and the emotions it awakens.

LEARNING TO LOVE

We do not have to be taught to care about ourselves. All living things—even one-celled animals—are driven to protect their own survival, and all naturally avoid or defend themselves against things that threaten them. All creatures likewise approach the things that are satisfying to them, turning toward food or warmth or the protection of shelter. We can observe the same thing in human beings from the moment of birth. If you stroke an infant's cheek, the baby will turn its head toward you in search of something to suckle. In this most elemental sense we are all born already self-concerned.

By contrast, the way we come to be concerned about others is through a long process of growth and experience. When we are very young our basic needs are met by other people. This not only ensures our survival, it also binds us to our caretakers in such a way that their mere presence is a powerful positive reward and their absence a cause of anxiety and distress. Human infants begin to love because they need the care of other people and because people respond to their needs. This attachment is the crucial beginning of their emotional development.

When those caretakers respond to the child reliably and warmly, the attachment is cemented and made secure, and it becomes the foundation for all later attachments. As those who care for the infant go on over years to engage the child's developing abilities with conversation and play and to treat him or her as important and valuable, they are forming the child's emerging sense of self. This does not require any particular plan or intention on the caretakers' part. Parents who cuddle and look after their babies do it as a matter of course and without thinking about it. This attentive caretaking is nonetheless vitally important because it is the basis of the child's later ability to recognize and relate to other selves.

It takes years to progress to the point where a young child realizes that other human beings are centers of experience in just the same way that the child is the center of his or her own experience. Children have to learn that other people hurt, get angry, and feel good or bad, and that these feelings are just as central and important to these people as the child's own feelings are to him or her. They learn this partly by observation and partly by having the experience of others narrated and named to them.

We do this all the time when children are very small, interpreting and giving words to other people's reactions so that the children can connect those reactions with their own feelings: "Suzy is crying because she fell down and scraped her knee. It hurts when that happens, doesn't it?" and so on. It is also one of the important functions of stories in a child's life. Where would we all be without the Alexanders who are having very bad days, and all their kindred? Even without putting it into words, the average parent of a preschooler knows all this perfectly well.

But the discovery that other people exist in this sense is a monumental turn for very young children. To maintain a real and steady awareness of others *as* others, at once like oneself and separate from oneself, is a huge accomplishment. From it comes the capacity to imagine and enter into another's experience and to treat that experience as important in its own right. This ability to empathize with others is what makes moral life possible. It makes the needs and claims of others not just an idea but a spur to action.

Many years ago, I heard from another parent that my first-grade son had been making fun of a child new to his school. I was surprised partly because he had himself been new to the school just the previous fall and I knew how keenly he had felt his initial isolation. It took only the obvious question, "How would you feel if someone did that to you?" to bring on tears and remorse. But this is not an idle question and asking it should not be merely a disguised reproach. It is an invitation into the world of other people, into the world of love and responsibility. It is in this sense, far more than in teaching manners or particular rules of behavior, that parents are their children's first and most important moral teachers.

The fact that our concern for others arises out of entering into their experience means that we are connected to other people first of all by sympathy and imagination. We first identify with their vulnerability, which we understand by analogy to our own. This fact has important implications for the character of human loves. If our ability to attend to the reality and importance of others is rooted in a kind of emotional identification with them, we will feel their grief or suffering as painful and their happiness as satisfying. This means that all our loves, including the most highly developed Christian love of neighbor, will include pleasure in the pleasure of those we come to love and a degree of sharing in their pain. It will include as well a desire to relieve their pain or extend their flourishing. This desire will prove to be an occasion of more joy or more suffering depending on whether or not it is possible for us to fulfill it. So the human experience of giving and receiving love has desire and pleasure woven into it as part of its texture. This is not to argue, as some have done, that all human loves are really pure desire, just disguised forms of selfishness that are really aimed only at our own comfort. And it certainly does not mean we ought to make decisions about our relationships based simply on what we as individuals find pleasant or painful at a given moment. But it does mean that human loves are not by their nature emotionally detached and disinterested in the sense used by philosophers; they are not unconcerned about and unconnected to our own feelings.

This means that these loves are never a matter of will and judgment and benevolence alone. Our emotions and our desires, and our suffering and rejoicing in and with others, remain bound up in them. Because human loves are passionate, they always include the self of the lover, his or her feelings and needs, as well as the needs and interests of the beloved. This is a basic and permanent feature of human loves, part of their richness and also part of their vulnerability to distortion.

THE PLEASURES OF CARETAKING

This intimate involvement of the self in human loves can be seen even in those loves that are most obviously centered on the other's needs. Think, for example, of the day-to-day care of infants. As anyone who has provided it knows, it is time and labor intensive and its tasks seem never-ending. It can certainly be physically exhausting, particularly for new parents who are still figuring out how to interpret and respond to the child's signals of distress. This may look like the ultimate one-sided relationship, where the giving is all on one side and the receiving all on the other. But that appearance is deceiving.

Under the right circumstances, where the child is healthy enough to respond to care and the caretaker has enough maturity and enough support (and often under circumstances much worse), even this one-sided relationship has a kind of mutuality built into it. Infants' ordinary responses of dependence, attachment, and trust powerfully reward the attention of those who care for them. There is intense satisfaction in being able to provide for the infant's needs. People who take care of infants get better at it, and as they do, the babies reach for and smile at their caretakers, which turns out to be enough to make the average grownup *want* to continue to offer care, and take a genuine pleasure in giving it.

As the bond between infant and caretaker develops, it is not really possible to sort out what is done purely "for the child's sake" and what is done for the pleasure of offering the care. It does not even make sense to make the distinction: it is responding to the child's need that gives the pleasure. Both the child and the caretaker, then, come to have a kind of need for each other and to take pleasure in each other, and the power of this bond grows with time. This is all good, part of the way in which our natural loves *are* natural. A caretaker or a child who did not develop such attachments, who did not take pleasure in them so that the relationship was a delight to both, would be worse off, not only practically but morally.

But the fact that there is a particular delight in being able to respond to children's needs means that there is also a kind of loss for caretakers as the need for care declines. As children grow up and need less and less constant interaction, it is natural to feel a little wistful about the babies they used to be. Because in our society it is more often mothers who spend the most time in infant care, this is more commonly a topic of conversation among women than among men. But I have also known male graduate students who were the stay-at-home parents who expressed the same half-sad, half-comic complaint: "She's started school! She hardly needs me anymore!"

The fact that this is said with humor and a hint of self-mockery is enough to show that there is no real problem here. But most parents negotiate this gradual loss of the complete intimacy of early childhood with some pain, and it is only the first of many such negotiations. First grade yields to middle school and high school, and before you know it your darling is announcing her intention to pursue graduate study at the London School of Economics. It takes genuine self-control to greet the news with the appropriate degree of enthusiasm when your inner response is, "But that's in London!"

The passionate attachments and deep satisfactions that are part of human loves sustain them and make them sweet. They also make them stumble sometimes. No honest parent can pretend to have gotten it right every time: to have given up gracefully every outgrown remnant of the child's onetime dependence, to have resolutely chosen the child's real interest over their own desires on every occasion. Accepting that even our love for our children is always a mixture of pure devotion to the child's welfare (I expect most parents really would run into a burning building after their kids) and our own delight in their care and company takes a certain humility and a certain kind of courage.

We have to take the risk of loving as well as we can, knowing and confronting the fact that it will not be nearly perfect. A friend of mine, perhaps influenced by his professional life as a Lutheran theologian, offers the following modest account of good parenting: "Good parents are those who give their kids the resources to recover from all the ways in which they have screwed them up; bad parents are those who don't. That's the whole difference."[14]

The point of all this is not to suggest that parents do not truly love their children because they fail to achieve the detached benevolence philosophers sometimes present as an ideal. (It would be a sad and bloodless version of a parent who did.) It is just to think about what difference it makes that human loves are those in which our emotions and our desires remain bound up. In light of that fact, we need to strike a sort of balance in our understanding.

NATURE AND GRACE

On one side, the continuing and vital engagement of the self with its own interests and desires is the hallmark of all natural loves, a mark of their springing from our basic character as social creatures. Our inclinations toward love and attachment are part of our fundamental orientation toward the good and even toward God. But according to the story Christians tell, what is natural is also fallen. It is damaged by our separation from God and thus caught up in the anxious and often disordered service of the self that marks all human beings.

The enduring presence of our own passions and needs in human loves brings with it possibilities that cannot be removed.

There is the possibility that self-absorption will conquer our concern for those we love, that self-deception will mislead us about the truth and the shape of love, even that an idolatrous readiness to make ourselves the whole center of meaning will turn our loves into something self-consuming and destructive. This means that the door to failure and distortion can never fully be closed. Even at their best, our loves remain vulnerable.

The illustrations I chose in the last section all come from the love of parents for children, but it would be easy to draw examples from other human relationships as well. Our loves for friends and romantic partners are equally freighted, carrying both powerful commitments to the good of the beloved, and powerful desires for the pleasures and comforts of the loving relationship. At our best we desire both the other person's good *and* the other person. We are always acting out of both of these desires, and in close personal relationships it is not unusual for them to conflict. Even the love that moves us to help neighbors in need is not immune from distortion. In the midst of our efforts to help, other interests can surface and turn to occasions for power seeking and pride. (The figure of Lady Bountiful, proud and condescending dispenser of blessings on the less fortunate, is a cultural symbol of such a corruption.[15])

The fruit of centuries of Christian reflection is this: we need to be schooled by teaching and practice in the love of neighbor, formed by our experience of the self-giving love of God, in order to love with wisdom and constancy. The "supernatural" love of charity helps us to sustain even our most human loves when they are costly or when something we naturally desire in them must be surrendered: the child grows up and moves away or the friend must be absent or the beloved must leave for the sake of some other good. But we will not come to such challenges easily or without feeling the pull of our own deep desires and our own painful attachments. Neither will we see clearly, choose rightly, or behave well every time. Love *is* hard and we do not always get it right. Nature is in need of grace.

Still, the ongoing presence in all human loves of the human person, the self with its needs and interests, its passions and its delights, is not just an opportunity for corruption. It is also a sign of something utterly fundamental and good about human existence. The desire for connection with others is deeply rooted in us, and the goodness of that desire remains even when we pursue that connection in self-defeating ways.

The recognition that we are oriented toward communion with others, that the basic stuff of human flourishing is relationship, is what allows Augustine to conclude that true self-love must be lived out in right relation to God and neighbor. If it is not, then it does not just break a rule or fail a moral test of unselfishness. It fails even to remain self-love, and becomes instead a kind of self-hatred. As all the sad statistics show, if we do not learn to love ourselves by loving others well, all our avid pursuit of happiness will in the end leave us isolated and deeply unsatisfied. Love really is what we were made for, and grace builds on and heals nature.

If our natural self-love leads us to relationship with others, and through them to relationship with their Creator, there is also another kind of movement: those who encounter God through the witness of scripture or the life of the Church or who are touched by the Spirit of God are led by their relationship with God into relationship with others. By command and teaching and example, by invitation and even by threat, relationship with God leads us to our neighbors in need. "Inasmuch as you did it to them, you did it to me" (Matt. 25:40) becomes the test of discipleship and the gateway of heaven.

The particular blessing of this movement outward from the Creator to the creature is the unlikely relationships it brings about. The Church itself is already a place of improbable friendships, but if it is faithful in its service it will also bring us into relationship with people we would not otherwise encounter and to whom we have no natural affinity. If our attraction to others whose gifts we admire can draw us toward the God who gives all gifts, it is also true that our connection with those to whom we are bound only by the love God commands can give us a taste of God's own love. For those who receive it, this is the sweetest and best of all gifts, the "pearl of great price" for which one would give all one had without hesitation. Nature too is fulfilled by grace.

COMING BACK TO CASES

An extended discussion about whether self-love is a problem or a duty or just a fact to be reckoned with may seem a long way from the practical concerns we started with: how we nurture and sustain and heal loving relationships. In reality I think it's not. I suspect that many of our public and passionate disagreements about how we ought to live stem from uncertainty about how our care for ourselves relates to or competes with our care for others or our faithfulness to God. (This is one way to understand the "culture wars" over divorce and abortion, among many other issues.)

I also think that our own most painful personal dilemmas arise out of struggles to find the right balance between self and others, between desires and obligations, between the things we want and the things we think we ought to do. The questions are endless and perplexing. What takes priority in a given situation? What kinds of sacrifices ought we to make for others' sake? Do we have duties to ourselves too? Can we make and keep commitments to spouses, to aging parents, to children without giving up altogether any claims for ourselves, any loyalty to our own flourishing? Is there such a thing as a proper self-regard?

I think of the story of an old and very dear friend. She was married for eighteen years to an attractive and gifted man who carried the baggage of a painful childhood scarred by his mother's abandonment. The marriage was like a long roller coaster ride, with times of intense mutual satisfaction but also recurrent bouts of terrible conflict and occasional explosions of violence. Their children were both deeply attached to their father and afraid of him, a toxic combination.

For my friend, even ordinary days were full of tension, because it was never possible to predict when things would spin out of control. Finances were always uncertain because her husband got and lost a succession of jobs and was cavalier about spending money. A series of emotional and in some measure sexual involvements with other women strained the basic trust of the marriage nearly to the breaking point. Finally, after my friend was launched on her own professional career, her husband began to undermine her work, using confidential information to sabotage her practice and place her clients at risk.

Through all the years of these escalating crises (I knew them as a couple for twelve years), my friend continually questioned what she should do and how she should decide. How was she to weigh her faithfulness to the promises of marriage against the actual problems of the relationship and its costs? She knew she had to do what she could to protect her children and she knew she had to consider her obligations to her husband and his welfare. But what about her own welfare? What about the emotional and eventual physical harm she suffered over these years as she developed stress-related diseases from constant anxiety? What about the pain she suffered? Did that count on the scale too? And how was she, who was anything but an objective bystander, supposed to weigh it all?

In fact, it was the attack on her professional life and on those she served that drove my friend to end the marriage. Looking back, she believes she should have done so earlier and spared her children (now young men) some of the turmoil of their growing up. (Of course there is no guarantee that a divorce in their childhood would not have inflicted just as much turmoil of a different kind.) Whether her judgment at the time was right or wrong, it is worth noting that it was the risks to others, her clients, that finally brought her to seek a divorce, and it is the harm to her children that now makes her regret waiting so long. She never has gotten clear about what she might owe herself, or how to weight a duty to herself in the balance of moral discernment.

I have already said that Christians have been far from unanimous about the love of self. It is no surprise then that the Christian tradition offers no guaranteed method for resolving such conflicts, no formula for arriving at the right answer in each case. But it does have important things to teach us all the same.

First, Christian teaching gives a very sober warning about the tendencies all human beings share and about the temptations to which we are all vulnerable. We are inclined to treat ourselves and our own feelings and needs as more compelling and central than the feelings and needs of others. We are likely to see situations in ways that favor our claims over those of others, and to find a way to construct what we ought to do to match more nearly what we want to do. We are, all of us, expert at these strategies, and these distorted forms of self-love remain a threat to our love for others and for God.

Second, in making Jesus the center, Christian tradition places before us a very demanding standard for real love. It includes profound loyalty even when it is costly, and even when the loyalty is not returned. If true love is seen when someone "lays down her life for a friend" (or even an enemy), then genuine sacrifice cannot be ruled out in advance as an aspect of such love.

At the same time, it is one thing to lay down your life and quite another to forfeit your soul. There is a sense in which love can call us to every sacrifice but this: that we place any other loyalty before our relationship with God. This means that we may not give up our own integrity as human beings made in God's image and called into friendship with God. We cannot allow ourselves to be used or violated for some cause less than God's own, or sacrificed on some other altar than God's. It is ironic but not surprising that American slaves in the nineteenth century found the resources for resistance in the Christian faith their masters had hoped would make them docile. Faithfulness does not always call for surrender.

Finally, the rich and ambivalent Christian tradition on self-love invites us to think more deeply and more seriously about who we are and what we genuinely need for fulfillment. It teaches us to pay attention to what gives us life and brings us joy, rather than having our desires dictated to us by media fantasies and our needs invented for us by advertising. In insisting that we are literally made to love God and one another, the Christian tradition on self-love offers us a genuine road to well-being and a way to love ourselves in truth.

After all we have seen, what remains is that self-love is both natural and fallen. It is a permanent feature of human beings, and it retains the power to foster illusions and to corrupt our loves so that they turn against us and devour themselves. But with all that, self-love's basic impulse toward the good is a part of how God made human beings, and part of how God calls us toward life and fullness. It has to be disciplined, corrected, and healed—not suppressed.

6

Love at Home:
Marriage and Parenthood

W hen I was in graduate school, our courses in Christian ethics dealt with love mostly in relation to the Great Commandment: that we should love God with all our heart and mind and strength, and our neighbors as ourselves. Lots of emphasis was put on the Bible's definition of the "neighbors" we were to love, and on how they included every person, known and unknown. This was natural enough in a department of religion, but over time I came to realize something: by focusing on our love for God and for neighbors-as-such, we kept our conversations and our thinking either "spiritual" (How do we love God?) or abstract. It was love in general that we were talking about.

This way of framing the conversation meant that the everyday relationships that occupy most of our time, those with friends or family members or coworkers, were thought of almost as exceptions. In fact, in the Protestant literature about Christian love, such particular connections are called "special relations." This terminology vaguely suggests that the normal relation between human beings is as strangers.

I suppose all this seemed odd to me because at the time my days were divided between the classroom and my life as a wife and the mother of young children. The daily round of dressing and feeding and bathing and playing with small girls, of negotiating school work and errands and chores and even the occasional conversation with my husband, was the "love" I knew most about. It wasn't especially spiritual, and it surely wasn't abstract. As much as I enjoyed my academic work, the connections between what we read and discussed in class and the loves that nourished and challenged me on a daily basis were not obvious.

But the connections between Christian reflection and day-to-day experience are there all the same. As the preceding few chapters have shown, our ordinary relationships with children and parents, friends and spouses, coworkers and the people next door provide constant evidence of the truth and importance of Christian insights about love. For example, we see all around us how central relationships are to our development and flourishing as human beings. We also see how failures in those relationships, both small and large, are marked by human tendencies toward self-centeredness and self-deception. Finally, human loves show all the signs of fragility and distortion that Christian tradition teaches us to expect, and this helps convince us of the need for something more than natural affection. We need a love grounded in something stronger and deeper than our own capacities to see truthfully and care faithfully, need it even to sustain the ordinary bonds that are the stuff of our daily lives.

So far we have been talking mostly in generalities, looking for illustration of Christian teachings about love in common human experience. In real life we have to love in particular, beginning with the people we see and know and have before us. The next few chapters focus more closely on our experience itself: on the challenges that confront us in our relationships, beginning with those nearest at hand.

PROMISING FOREVER: ROMANTIC LOVE AND THE PROBLEM OF MARRIAGE

In my first year of college teaching, I was responsible for a general course in morality required of all undergraduates at a large Catholic university. Part of the curriculum I inherited from my predecessor was a unit on sex, marriage, and family life, always a

lively topic in a room full of eighteen- to twenty-year-olds. Many
issues emerged over our weeks of conversation, but the discussion I remember most vividly was prompted by the remarks of a
young woman from India. In the middle of a discussion about
the ethics of dating and what our rather outmoded textbook
called "courtship," she announced her intention to return home
upon the completion of her degree and marry a young man
chosen for her by her parents, a boy she had met only once.

Her classmates were astounded—and appalled. The custom
of arranged marriage struck them as outlandish, even barbaric.
She was bombarded with incredulous questions: How could you
give up the most important decision of your life? How can your
parents tell you who to love? How can you marry a stranger?
What if you can't stand each other? Her plan seemed nothing
short of crazy to them, and they were not shy about saying so.

I was prepared to intervene, but in fact the student did not
need my help. She replied that she had been living in a college
dorm in the United States for two years and had observed all
around her what they called dating. It seemed to her altogether
absurd. You are eighteen or nineteen, she told them; you have no
experience of the world but you propose to choose a life partner on the basis of campus popularity and hormones. Meanwhile
you experiment with sex, and you are lucky if all that happens is
that your feelings get trampled on.

How much better, she argued, to trust the judgment and
experience of the parents who know and love you, who want
only what is best for you. Her parents, she informed them, had
watched this young man from his childhood. They knew his family
and his upbringing and his religious views, they knew his plans and
prospects for the future, and they were in a much better position
than she to predict that theirs would be a happy and successful
union.

Naturally her peers were unconvinced and they produced
what they considered the trump card: But you are not in love
with this man! She was not impressed. What you call "in love,"
she insisted, is just sexual excitement and infatuation, and it passes
as quickly as it comes. We will share our lives and get to know

one another deeply, she explained, and we will learn to love each other. And that is where the conversation rested, with each side firmly persuaded that they had the best of the argument.

Although none of those college freshmen and sophomores may have recognized it, my Indian student surely had the weight of history on her side. The idea that the important social institution of marriage should rest on a foundation as unpredictable as romantic attraction, even the relatively more stable and considered attractions of full-fledged adults, is a recent one. When it was seriously put forward by intellectuals in the nineteenth century it was seen as quite radical, and it did not become part of general expectations in our society until the twentieth century was well under way. In some ways the social history of the West in the last two hundred years could be written in terms of gradual shifts in the understanding of marriage: from a social arrangement for the control of sex and the rearing of children to a practical partnership to a love affair between two individuals to which official public recognition is given after the fact.

Now, of course, the assumption is firmly in place that we naturally ought to marry the person with whom we fall in love. Our novels and movies and music celebrate narratives in which love conquers all, and our popular romances are much more likely to be comedies than to be tragedies. Romantic attraction is expected to serve not only as the force that *brings* couples together but also as the glue that *holds* them together. And that, as we noted in an earlier chapter, creates an enormous social problem. For as powerful and delightful as romantic love can be, it is not necessarily lasting. Even while it lasts, the intensity and drama of *eros* may not provide the practical security people need to flourish in the long term, or a safe and reliable context for the long-term project of having and raising children.

In making romantic love the central or even the sole bond on which marriage rests, we have taken a kind of love rooted in freedom, choice, and spontaneous delight and made it the basis for a relationship fenced in by obligations and intended for permanence. We make promises and then must rely on our feelings to enable us to keep them. Yet how can anyone promise to feel in a particular way ten or twenty or even fifty years in the future? And what are we to do if our feelings change and we confront the prospect of long years of—what? Dutiful companionship, full of regrets? Deception and pretense as we try to hide the death of delight and desire from the person who shares our bed? Polite coexistence without real intimacy? With such bleak possibilities in view, no wonder people who find that romantic love has died so often conclude there is no decent alternative but to divorce, as amicably as possible, with as little damage as possible.

The first problem with this understandable conclusion is that (as a half century of experience has shown) even the minimum of damage turns out to be quite a bit more than anyone expected. This is true for the former spouses, who often find themselves carrying a load of guilt, grief, and anger as well as deep doubts about the kind of love of which they are capable. It is even truer for any children born of the marriage. For them, the dissolution of any family life short of open warfare comes as a terrible blow. About this the majority of sociologists, psychologists, economists, and educators agree. On any measure of success and stability, well-being or life satisfaction, the children of divorce show significant losses when compared to their peers from intact homes, and those effects are long lasting.

The second problem is that more often than not, divorce offers no permanent resolution to the problems it aims to solve. Obviously it ends the marriage between the former partners. But if there are children, it does not end the couple's relationship or their need to collaborate in the areas of money and child-rearing, which are among the most common areas of conflict between spouses. In fact, it ensures years of negotiations and settlements as the children's needs and circumstances change over time and new arrangements for sharing responsibilities must be formalized.

Regardless of any relationship with the former spouse, the now-divorced partners are very likely to remarry. They go looking for the renewed excitement of being in love, and for the warmth and stability of a lasting partnership, the life pattern that people generally find to be the most rewarding. Unfortunately for those who remarry seeking the happiness that eluded them in the first relationship, the odds of their succeeding in these second or subsequent marriages are even lower than they were the first time. The likelihood is high that the partners will face another failure and another painful dissolution, and graver doubts about their own capacity to love and be loved. We may not be very good at living without marriage, but that doesn't mean we know how to make it work.

It does not take a great deal of historical insight to understand why this pattern has emerged. On the one hand, the powerful practical forces that used to keep couples together—the fear of social stigma and the economic impossibility for most people of surviving as single parents—have weakened considerably. At the same time, expectations of personal fulfillment have risen, particularly for women. This has changed our judgments about what is an acceptable quality of relationship and an acceptable level of individual satisfaction. It is easier than it has ever been to conclude that a particular marriage is a bad bargain and that one is better off without it. From there the natural next step seems to be to try again to find a new and more satisfying romantic partner.

The trouble is that this strategy treats the failure of the marriage as a mere happenstance, something that comes about incidentally and has no bearing on the future. But there is much, including a divorce rate that hovers around 50 percent, to suggest that the problem is more systemic than that. It may simply be the case that the bond of romantic love that we are relying on to keep married couples together is not well suited to the task.

Consider the elements we associate with romantic love, particularly with the "falling in love" phase that frequently leads to proposals of marriage. To begin with, we expect sexual appeal, that awakened interest that makes us aware of someone as a man or woman and a potential romantic partner. We expect attraction, that combination of personal taste and chemistry that turns our general openness to someone into romantic attachment. As the relationship builds, we look for excitement, the sense of the mere presence of the other as intensely rewarding. It is here that we use words like *magic* or *intoxication* to convey our sense of the uniqueness of this relationship. By this point there is often a degree of idealization of the partner, a selectivity of attention to their real qualities that is reflected in popular proverbs like "love is blind."

All of this is accompanied by liking and mutual enjoyment, but it is also flavored with novelty, sexual excitement, and the profound personal affirmation of being found attractive and desirable. As trust grows and confidences are exchanged, as more and more of the self is shared and welcomed, the simple sense of being vitally important to someone, the center of his or her attention, is a powerful bond in itself. Often the hardest aspect of breaking off a romantic attachment is giving up that sense of being the center of the universe for some other person. Many weddings have gone forward despite doubts because that loss was too much to face.

None of this is meant to disparage the power of romantic attraction or to make light of the depth and seriousness that romantic loves can have. Such loves really can give us a taste of what unqualified devotion to another person might look like, and create in us a readiness for genuine self-giving. At their best they can make us more alive to the possibilities of human existence, more grateful, attentive, and generous. In that way they can serve as a school for the wider loves of friendship, affection, and charity. But it is worth noting that the circumstances of marriage make it hard to sustain many of the feelings and experiences we associate with romantic love.

To start with the most superficial element, sexual appeal is particularly vulnerable to changes in appearance. Some of these come with time and some come just from the fact that spouses see each other at all sorts of times, at their worst as well as at their best, and no longer only when they are dressed and groomed to be pleasing. Even an ordinary amount of maturity would be enough to reckon with this if it weren't for all the other challenges. But there are others.

Married life makes it harder for the partners to be attentive to each other, partly because the tasks and pressures of grown-up life crowd out time to focus on the partner (hence the reams of good advice written for couples about how important it is to make time for the relationship). However, this is not just a practical problem to be remedied by better time management. Some of the natural motivation for taking time and paying real attention fades.

Routine replaces spontaneity, and the spouse you see every day is so far from being novel, so much part of the landscape of your daily life, that it may become difficult to stop and really see him or her at all. Likewise, the emotional power of your partner's interest in and attraction to you fades as well. As the common phrase has it, you take this person "for granted," and the very familiarity of domestic exchanges of sex and affection can cause them to lose the capacity to move us and nourish us. The "of course"-ness of marriage is, from the point of view of romance, deadly.

Finally, we have said that romance typically includes a degree of idealization of the partner, even a measure of illusion about who this other person really is. These romanticized images are matched by the illusions we all have about ourselves. But over time the nature of marriage is fatal to all such illusions, and here is where the most serious threat lies. The practical challenges that take a toll on marriages routinely include problems at work, concerns about money, and friction over dividing tasks. Deeper and more difficult struggles arise over how to handle issues with children and how to harmonize the long-term needs and goals of two adults when these diverge. These issues are things that both partners have a huge stake in, and the conflicts that emerge are sometimes intense and painful. Put simply, with time we discover that marriage is hard.

Dealing with this whole range of problems will inevitably reveal new things about who we and our spouses turn out to be, including faults and weaknesses and characteristic sins. We learn how this person behaves when he is really angry, what she does when she is afraid, how he acts when deeply hurt. (Most people behave rather badly under these circumstances.) Given enough time we will also discover all the baggage our partner carries from unresolved childhood issues, and run head on into all the destructive patterns inherited from the home in which she or he grew up. (We also get to learn the same things about ourselves as we come to see ourselves through our spouse's eyes. It is hard to say which is worse.)

It is no wonder that married people at times find themselves sharing a bed with someone who has become something of a stranger—or something of an enemy. Now I want to be careful here, because I have spoken to couples who profess to have no idea what I am talking about, who insist that they have never come to wrenching conflicts in their relationship and do not find marriage hard. I have no reason to doubt them. You may have had the same experience. Still, I have to say that all the couples I have known well enough and long enough to have any real knowledge of their marriages have faced times of real and some-times prolonged pain and difficulty: times when they could find little or nothing left of the feelings toward and perceptions of their partners that brought them into the relationship. Certainly my husband and I have been through such times in our thirty years together.

And here is where we confront the limits of romantic love. What are we to do when the desire, the delight, the attraction are gone? How about when they are replaced by anger and disap-pointment, by grief and distrust, or perhaps worst of all, by blank indifference and desperate loneliness? How do we go on in a relationship when the love that brought it into being seems, to all appearances, to have died?

WAITING FOR A RESURRECTION

To these questions I am going to give responses that come out of the wisdom and long teaching tradition of the Church and out of my own years of experience, both personal and pastoral. But before I do, I want to be very clear about one thing: noth-ing I will say adds up to a promise or a guarantee that if you just do the right things, follow the right steps, even pray the right prayers, things will be fixed. They may not be. All I can offer is a way forward, a way to make a possibility and a space for healing.

There is no certainty that healing will come. That depends on the grace of God, which can be counted on, but it also depends on the freedom and the limitations of human beings, and these cannot be determined in advance. This means that even to try involves a risk. It requires courage, for it is possible that trying will only prolong a terrible process and come to nothing, except for this: you will know that you have done all that was possible for you to do, and that may help you find peace and forgiveness in the end.

The first word to be said is also the hardest to hear, and the hardest to act on. It is simply that one must wait. This sounds easy unless you have ever experienced the profound pain of a marriage from which love seems gone forever, and in which every moment is a reminder of what is lost, like attending a perpetual wake. The impulse to flee is overwhelming. You want to distract yourself, to devote your time and energy to something else, to put the whole thing behind you and get on with a life that doesn't feel so much like death.

This, I suspect, is what lures so many people whose marriages are in real trouble into affairs. It is not that they do not "know better" in some sense: even in secular and post-sexual-revolution America, something like 90 percent of those asked will say that adultery is wrong. Neither is it chiefly that people need a sexual substitute for the estranged spouse. It is just that the feelings of rejection and failure are so acute that it is hard to resist taking comfort in the arms of someone who finds you desirable and lovable when you are likely to feel neither.

In such cases infidelity is more the result than the cause of the trouble, but it brings a whole new set of issues in its train. It does not always make recovery impossible; I have seen more than one marriage weather even this crisis and emerge stronger and more deeply grounded than before. But the scars are deep and lasting, and the process of healing is difficult; certainly it cannot be counted on. Adultery can be the blow that shatters the last remnant of trust and closes the door on any future.

But it is not enough to resist the desire to run from a painful situation and to avoid seeking comfort in another relationship.

The kind of patience that makes the recovery of a marriage possible involves hard work. The work of waiting is not just to mark time but to use the time to see our situation and our role in it differently. Very often that means giving up the story we have been telling ourselves about how we got here in the first place: the one in which we are largely innocent and our spouse bears most if not all the blame.

One of the hardest lessons of life is coming to recognize that we do not simply see whatever is in front of us. We see what we expect to see, what we are prepared to see, and especially what we want to see. This is why two parties to a dispute or two drivers in an accident so often cannot agree on what happened. It is not so much that they are being deliberately dishonest as that they saw what they were ready to see (their side of the story) and that is what they remember. Memory, like the vision on which it depends, is something we construct, not something we simply record.

This is not a new observation. At the start of the thirteenth century, medieval philosopher Thomas Aquinas wrote that the central moral virtue from which all the others flow is prudence. At its heart, prudence is the ability to see the world as it is and thus to navigate a path toward the good. Because finding a way into the future involves understanding the past, Aquinas argued, part of prudence is *memoria,* the capacity for truthful memory. So remembering, it turns out, is a moral activity, and a moral challenge.

This is easy enough to see when two people have an argument. Each of them is ready with a story about who started it, what happened next, who said what and did what, and whose fault the whole thing was. Each person believes firmly what she or he is saying, but the stories rarely match. If they wait a while, until they are no longer angry and upset, the accounts may start to come together. Often the process of making up after a fight involves exactly this: coming to a shared story about what happened that both people can accept.

On a much larger and more serious scale, this is part of what is called for when a marriage has come apart and both spouses feel aggrieved and angry—or worse, when the alienation is too great for them to feel much of anything. This is a great deal easier to say than it is to do, but part of making reconciliation possible is opening ourselves up to a new story, one in which we have hurt and disappointed as much as we have *been* hurt and disappointed.

This does not necessarily mean declaring yourself to be in the wrong when you really don't see it that way. It is only necessary to realize that your partner is suffering too, and that people tend to behave badly when they are in pain. A little bit of reflection may then make you wonder whether your being in pain has led you to behave badly as well. That can be enough for a beginning, and it may take quite a bit of time to get even this far.

Here is one of the places where the teaching and disciplines of Christian life may help in the hard work of sustaining and healing loves that are damaged. Unfortunately it is easy enough to recite the prayers of confession out of Sunday's worship bulletin every week and still defend one's own innocence in every particular case. But if Christians take their regular confessions of sin and weakness with any seriousness at all, it can help them acknowledge that they are probably not wholly without fault in what has happened to put their marriages at risk. And it can also remind them of something even more basic: that they should never have expected their marriages to succeed on the basis of their own goodness or that of their partner. Instead, Christian marriage rests entirely on both spouses' willingness to offer and receive forgiveness.

The last thing that can come of having the patience to wait for healing in a marriage is something we touched on in an earlier chapter. Sometimes the quiet and perspective offered by a time of waiting can provide an opportunity for the recovery of vision. This time I mean not a more balanced vision of our own role in the problems we confront, but rather the vision of our partner that drew us in the first place. Here is another aspect of truthful memory: the willingness to keep open the door to a past in which love was awakened and responded to in freedom and delight. This is particularly important when what has happened in the marriage is not some focused conflict or some

grave violation of trust but rather the long, slow erosion of attention and presence.

Here I am drawing on the ideas of Margaret Farley, a Roman
Catholic moral theologian who has written a profoundly illuminating book about personal commitments.[1] In it she talks about
the conditions that enable us to remain present and engaged in
our most central and challenging commitments, including marriage. One of those conditions is something she names "relax-
ation of heart."[2] This is a condition of waiting in hope, sustained
by memory, for a renewal and recovery of what we once saw and
knew and responded to: the vision of the partner that called forth
love and commitment in the beginning.

It requires patience and openness, with all the effort they may
entail. But it also requires stillness, and trust, and a surrender of
control, for the love we are seeking to rekindle cannot be insisted
on. It must be reawakened in us, called forth anew from a heart
that gives it freely, knowing the risk. It is a resurrection we are
waiting for. But of course, Christians believe in resurrection.

If everything I have proposed so far sounds hard, costly, and
lonely, it often is. In fact, it is *so* hard and lonely that I cannot
really imagine finding in oneself the resources to manage it. From
my own experience, and from the experiences shared with me
by many others, I would say that the ability to wait and work for
the renewal of love in a marriage when it seems to have died
depends on resources wholly beyond one's own. It depends on
the strength and comfort and constant companionship of God.

It is very hard to talk about this without sounding pious
and sappy, like bad religious poetry, so I will put it as plainly as
I can. Everyone I know who has tried to walk this path reports
the same thing: that for a time, at least, when their own hope
and strength were exhausted, when they had nothing else to
hang onto, they survived on the continual presence and almost
palpable support of God. Let me be clear and say that I am not
talking about mysterious voices or miracles, special divine inter-
vention, or anything at all spectacular. I am talking about being
able to stop when it seems impossible to go on and simply ask
for help to see the path and for the strength to walk on it. I am

talking about resting in the certainty that God will provide sustenance and make a way forward even when that way cannot be seen. I am talking about the trust that God will lead you into a life that is full and worthwhile, whether in this marriage or without it, even if its shape cannot now be imagined. That last comment may seem strange. All along I have been talking about how to preserve and restore a marriage in trouble. Why would I now want to introduce the idea that one might do without it? It is partly because I have found that if a person is going to take the risk of trying to sustain a difficult relationship, it is important that his or her whole life and being not rest on it. Otherwise the risk becomes too great to bear. But there is another, more important reason for such a reservation.

God alone is to be the center of a human existence, the One a person cannot live without. Neither a spouse nor any other human being can or should bear the weight of being the center of the universe for another person, and the essential wholeness of a human being cannot rest on anything other than God. This is not only a religious requirement: it is also the only way to have a whole human self to be shared in love with another. It is this wholeness that enables someone to wait in faith, hope, and charity, and to remain open to a renewal of love and commitment. And if it should unhappily come to it, this same wholeness is what enables that person to follow Paul's advice (1 Cor. 7:15) to let a partner who decides finally to cut the cord to go in peace.[3]

THE MORAL CHALLENGE
OF PARENTHOOD

Whole aisles of any large bookstore are devoted to manuals about parenting. These range from advice and instructions to the pregnant mother to books promising to help parents weather the storms of adolescence. They offer (variously) to teach one how to raise children who are healthy, polite, and responsible, have good self-esteem, stay in church, or get into Harvard. What these books have in common is that they aim to help the parent shape the child, to bring about the best outcome in the child's physical, emotional, intellectual, and spiritual well-being. Many of these books are good and praiseworthy efforts, and there is doubtless much useful information and sound advice in them. But none of them pays much attention to what it takes to shape a good *parent,* or to how hard it is to be one.

Here I don't mean the material difficulties of child-rearing (how expensive it is to raise and educate a child through twenty plus years) or its practical challenges (how hard it can be to keep a child safe and healthy in a world of risks and temptations). I don't mean the physical effort of constant care or the emotional toll of worry or even the real suffering when a child is sick or unhappy or in trouble, great as these can be. I mean the specifically *moral* challenges of parenting: how hard it is to become a person with the qualities of character it takes to exercise such enormous power in the life of another human being, and do it well.

Some of these moral challenges we recognize implicitly. We talk about the patience required to care for young children, for example, or the sheer stamina it takes to fulfill the unending tasks of child-rearing. Mothers in particular are powerful cultural symbols of devotion and unselfishness, to the point that some of our ideals of motherhood look a lot like the ideals of martyrdom in earlier centuries. We have clearly established the idea that one must love a great deal to be a parent, and that good parents love their children intensely.

We give less attention to the fact that good parents must love wisely as well as greatly. For instance, we don't probe very deeply into the habits of mind and heart that make it possible to sort out what a child actually needs at a given time from what he or she may want. (Good parenting requires judgment, a combination of clear-sightedness, confidence, and flexibility, that an older moral tradition called prudence.) We do not focus much on the self-awareness and self-restraint it takes to separate one's own feelings and desires in this relationship from what is best for the child, even as his or her needs change over time. (Good parenting requires self-knowledge and emotional maturity.) Putting all this into action can take considerable self-control.

Many years ago, when my own first child was still a toddler, I sat on a playground with another mother on a summer afternoon. The other woman was a little older and had a five-year-old son about to enter kindergarten. As our children played in the sandbox and on the swing set, we talked about a crisis in her household several months before. Her son had climbed up onto a kitchen chair, fallen, and fractured his skull. His injury was not as severe as it might have been, and it now appeared that he would suffer no long-term effects. After many weeks of careful monitoring, he was free to run and play again. Nevertheless, the whole thing had been harrowing and his mother was just beginning to feel like she could breathe once more.

While we were talking, her little boy called out to her to watch him go down the slide. She smiled and waved at him and called back that she was looking. I remember being surprised, because this slide was a grand old classic model, with a metal ladder reaching eight feet in the air. I expected her to tell him that he couldn't go, that it was too high, that he might fall. Instead she sat there steadily, smiling and encouraging. It was only when I saw the white knuckles of her hands gripping the arms of her lawn chair that I realized she was desperately nervous and doing her very best to hide her anxiety from her little boy. He climbed up and sailed down, thoroughly delighted with himself—and unafraid. It was her judgment that he was ready for this boy-sized triumph, even if she was not, and she kept her fears out of sight. I thought at the time that I could not have done it.

Parents are constantly called on to make risky judgments about what their children are ready to try, balancing the possibility of harm against the child's need to gain skill and confidence in negotiating the world. Making such judgments and acting according to them is not easy. But it is an example of the basic moral challenge of parenting, which is to use a greatly unequal power generously and consistently, for the child's good and not for our own comfort. It takes a whole constellation of virtues to manage that, a set of dispositions and skills that for most of us are still very much under construction when our children arrive. So it's not surprising that any honest parent can think of any number of times when he or she has failed this test in one way or another.

Teaching young children how to behave and responding when they behave badly is one area that constantly challenges parents. I know there were many occasions when I could not muster the energy for another struggle with my toddlers and so turned a blind eye to some infraction that really should have been corrected. On the other hand, like all parents, I suppose, I can think of instances when my discipline of a child had far more to do with my own frustration or fatigue than with what was reasonable to expect of the child or appropriate as a means of correction. Many of these occurrences are minor lapses and become important only when they form a pattern of negligence or harshness. But even a single occasion can be powerful.

I remember an afternoon when my ordinarily sweet and compliant middle daughter, then about ten, seemed to me just obstinately defiant and disrespectful. I cannot recall any more what the issue was. Some kind of discipline was certainly in order. But instead of figuring out what was behind her uncharacteristic behavior or even just waiting until my own emotions were under control, I did something I almost never did and gave her an openhanded slap on the thigh. The point is not that all physical punishment is always wrong. (Good parents disagree deeply about that.) The point is that I struck her in anger, and too hard. I was not really acting as a parent; I was just losing my temper with a little girl. I take some comfort in the fact that my daughter does not even remember the incident, but I think I will never forget it. The memory still makes me wince after more than a decade.

But there is more to parenting than taking good care of children and making good decisions on their behalf—more even than acting with maturity and self-restraint, though all these are needed. It is not enough to do all the things children require, to feed and look after, supervise and educate them. A great deal depends on *how* we do what we do. For both the parents' sake and the child's, good parenting must include taking delight in our children. Children need to grow up with the feeling that it is *good news* that they are in the world, and that their parents are happy to have them to care for.

We don't think very often about what enables people not merely to fulfill their responsibilities as parents but to do so freely and joyfully. But parents who cannot do that, who experience the years of raising their children largely in terms of the sacrifices they require or the constraints they represent, are likely to have stored up a fair amount of resentment by the time those children are grown. They are also likely to have given their children a sense of being a burden that will generate a matching resentment in them. It is easy to imagine the outcome: relationships that are strained and dutiful at best, with a sense of grievance and disappointment on both sides.

I think of a family I have known since childhood. The parents were a pleasant and well-groomed couple who maintained an immaculate house and a tidy garden and raised remarkably polite and well-behaved children, a daughter and a son. (As kids we always got extra lectures on good behavior before we visited them.) The household was never unpleasant and I never saw any evidence of serious conflict there. But it was never an especially warm or welcoming place for us either. As a child I could not imagine the scenes of silliness or roughhousing that were common at my house happening there. Everything was too neat.

The couple is older now, in their early seventies. Their children, now middle-aged, remain polite and somewhat formal. Both live far away from their parents, although they visit when holidays roll around. The parents complain that it is not often enough, and that even when they come their children do not seem to want to be there. They say they always expected grandchildren, but neither of their children has had children of their own. Their children say (privately) that their parents never really seemed to enjoy having children around, and they always felt like they were something of an inconvenience. Neither daughter nor son wanted children because to them they seemed to be too much bother. On both sides there is a vague sense of regret.

Sometimes the idea that parenting is a sacrifice is not merely implied but made explicit. I once knew a young woman whose mother had been a professional dancer before her marriage and had left her career and her art to raise a large family. As a mother she was exemplary in many ways. She gave her kids plenty of attention, chose good schools for them, and saw that they enjoyed the full complement of lessons, sports teams, and scouting activities.

But she never for a moment let her children forget what she had given up for them. When I knew her, this young woman was expending enormous amounts of time, money, and effort trying to establish a career in ballet, an art form for which her body type and her physical talents were not especially well-suited. She knew her chances of success were nearly nonexistent. Still, she could not give up her struggle; she somehow had to make up for what her mother had forfeited.

So it is possible for parents to remain self-centered in a way that distorts the parent-child relationship. Parents may insist on fitting their children into a mold shaped by the parents' own priorities and dreams—anything from unfulfilled personal goals to a need for order—and they can do it whether the fit is a good one or not. In the dynamics of family life, it seems that the center of gravity remains firmly in the parents' lives. The child represents a kind of force that pulls the parents off center, a force they try to counteract by getting the child to conform to a role that provides for the parents' needs rather than the child's flourishing. Through all this the child's basic needs are met, the parents' responsibilities are fulfilled, and no one could call these parents neglectful. But there is no sense of liberty in the giving, and thus no joy in the receiving.

On the other hand, it is possible to err in the opposite direction as well. Rather than being *self*-absorbed, one can be absorbed so completely into the role of parent that one loses any identity or purpose apart from that relationship. This is the sort of thing we mean when we say that someone "lives for" his or her children. The trouble is that this approach so often slides into living *through* them.

When that happens, the children's accomplishments are the parents' means of fulfillment, the justification and validation of their existence. The result is that this manner of parenting, like the last, turns into a form of constraint. The children are not free to experiment or to fail, because the parents' identity and sense of worth are riding on the children's performance. (Think of the adolescents who have to get into an Ivy League school to prove their parents' success.) They cannot choose a career or a life path that the parent does not value, because they must make good on the parents' investment. (I still remember the familial fireworks when one bright young cousin announced her intention to major in ceramics.) Neither are they entirely free to grow up and go off into the world to pursue a life of real independence. If they did, what would become of Mother or Dad? For the children who do break away and establish an appropriately separate adult life, there is often a high price to pay in recrimination on one side—"After all I've done for you!"—and guilt on the other.

FINDING THE RESOURCES

What this long string of examples aims to show is that to be a good parent takes a considerable degree of personal wholeness. It takes humility to be a deeply invested participant in another's life and to exercise enormous power and authority in the other's development without simply treating that life as a means to one's own fulfillment. But it also takes a secure sense of personal identity and worth to offer years of care and service to someone else while maintaining a fundamental respect for one's own independent value and integrity as well as for the value and integrity of the child and the adult she or he is to become.

Only such a balance will allow a parent to pour out time and energy and passion on someone day after day and year after year and have it retain the quality of a gift freely given and not a debt to be repaid. Only that kind of wholeness makes it possible to care so deeply and take such delight in another human being while retaining a sense of being a person in one's own right, with other commitments to make and other callings to honor.

This is crucial because, unlike our other primary relationships, the relationship between parents and children is not successful unless it eventually becomes obsolete. The emotional bond between parent and child endures, of course, but the dependency, the vast difference in power, the *need* that forms the relationship in its beginning must all fade away. To do the job of a parent well is to help bring into being a person who no longer needs parenting in a primary sense, who can someday go into the world joyfully and confidently to make a life in which the parent recedes into a relatively minor role. Perhaps the central virtue of parenting is the kind of generosity that allows one to welcome and celebrate that day when it comes.

By now this long catalogue of the moral challenges of parenting and the qualities needed to meet them may have convinced you that no one should attempt it. Anything that requires patience, constancy, judgment, self-knowledge, maturity, self-control, humility, wholeness, and generosity is evidently a job for saints and not ordinary mortals. No wonder the response of brand new parents is so often joy, followed immediately by panic.

But all of this is not an impossible ideal of parental perfection or a counsel of despair. It is a way of fleshing out what it means to say that love is hard, and showing that the loves that are most central and intimate and powerful in our lives are not made any easier by being so close at hand. It also helps to make clear what was meant in the last chapter, that although grace builds on nature, nature also requires grace.

The profound natural attachment of parents to their children provides the intensity of parental love, but it does not in itself provide the wisdom. We really do need more than our own resources to get it right, to manage with some consistency the decades of energy and passion, careful judgment, and free self-giving that it takes to nurture another full-fledged human being into health and independence.

Reflections like these take us back to the discussion in Chapter Three of the things in us that limit our ability to love and of the practices that strengthen it. Here I want to suggest that those who aim to devote themselves to the long and happy labor of raising children need deep wells on which to draw. They need places to rest and be refreshed, to be fed and nurtured themselves if they are to feed and nurture the children who look to them. There must be places where they can lay aside the burden of judgment and the appearance of confidence and strength their children will expect, settings in which they may acknowledge all the doubts and uncertainties that attend the business of parenting and admit their own worry and confusion.

To some extent, such support can come from wider family networks and from other parents with whom the stories, laughter, and tears that come with parenthood can be shared. But people need even more than this if they are to grow into men and women with the wisdom to be good parents. They need not only the idea of God but also God as a living presence from whom they take their calling to nurture and protect and to whom they ultimately confide it.

Concretely, parents need the practices of worship to remind them of the limits of their own control, and they need the Communion table to remind them of their own need for nourishment. They need the continual practice of confession to remind them of the possibility of and need for forgiveness when they do the wrong thing. And they need One to whom they can go when what confronts them is beyond their resources, when grief overwhelms or despair threatens.

Ultimately they need to be able to entrust their children to the one Parent whose love never falters and whose wisdom is absolute, for the real sacrifice of parenting is not its labor or its expense or the permanent sense of being on twenty-four-hour call. It is the risk of having your heart broken by caring deeply and forever about the welfare of someone you cannot finally keep safe. It takes courage as well as wisdom to love a mortal human being, and never more than in the case of one's own child.

I hesitate even to raise this most terrible prospect, the loss of a child, because like most parents I can hardly bear to contemplate it. But of course there are parents who must find a way to live with such a devastating blow, and it seems a sort of cowardice not even to name this possibility. At the same time, only a fool would try to offer comfort in the face of such a catastrophe, not having faced it herself. I do not offer comfort, then, but just a call to those suffering with overwhelming grief not to imagine that they are forever beyond the reach of the One who can.

What follows is the text of a letter written to parents whose daughter had been killed in a car wreck some months before:

Dear Ray and Sally:

I think of you both every day, and pray for you, and hug you at a distance, and know that I cannot imagine what it is like for you right now, just getting through the days. Everyone says that holidays are the worst, all occasions that mark and measure out the time, and what has changed and what is lost. But since these days have to be gotten through one way or another, I wanted to write something that has been on my mind recurrently as Christmas approaches.

I am afraid that you will feel like you don't belong in the world right now: that Christmas is for other people, people whose worlds are still intact and who can still imagine that they are safe. I want to say that in fact Christmas is for you, indeed always and especially for you, and for all the heartsick and those who are near to despair. It is for this very thing that Jesus came and is coming and comes ever and again to this lost and broken planet, to bring God's life to a world that is otherwise mortally wounded and on its way to death. For that is the truth hiding behind the loud recorded music and the tinsel and the multicolored lights: that we are all of us dying, fast or slow, soon or late, visibly or invisibly, and we cannot help ourselves. That fact was probably harder to hide from in the world into which Jesus was born; there was less of the noise and glitter, and death was closer to most people in both time and space since they died younger and washed and buried their own dead.

But the whole news of that first Christmas night was just this astonishing thing: that God has refused to abandon us to death and has instead come after us. He sent Jesus as a kind of rescue party out into the world of flesh, into the world of being born and dying, to share our lives and to offer us some of God's own life, which is real life and goes on forever. And the shape of that divine life is love.

It was love that brought Jesus, and love that he showed and taught, and love he told us to hold out for in the face of the fear and hatred that death inspires in us. It was love like you held Kyla in and taught her to offer to others. The trouble is that in a world like ours, where death seems still to reign, love is costly, and what it costs is simply everything. It means that you risk a broken heart. In fact, if you live long enough, you can count on one. I wish I could tell you the pain will go away, but it won't. Not altogether. But it will change, become softer and more bearable, and leave your hearts tender forever. And finally it will be vindicated, because the only thing that goes on and is redeemed and kept forever in God's hand is love. And so you and Kyla will embrace again in the end.

But the wait is hard and the suffering is real, and there is nothing wrong with grieving. Others can share it with you but no one can bear it for you. What you do get is companionship: your friends, your family, each other—and that greatest of all companions, God himself. For whenever you feel like no one can know, remember that God is a parent too, and a parent who suffered the death of a child. There is no cry that cannot be heard and understood and borne by that great heart.

So, dear people, hold on tight to the blessing of Christmas, and to the One who was born so that we might all be done with dying forever. God bless.

Sondra

7

Love Freely Chosen: Friendship

It had been an awful week. As usual there were too many things to get done and not enough time to do them. But this week a range of personal, job, and academic pressures had converged to make every member of my family anxious, frustrated, and irritable. By Wednesday I knew it was coming, and on Sunday night one of the storms of emotion that are the occasional backdrop to family life broke. I was caught up in my usual role of family mediator and referee, a role I hate but cannot seem to put down. When Monday dawned, I already felt exhausted and dispirited. I got through a seemingly endless day, dealing with a series of mishaps and complaints. All the while I was mulling over the previous week's events and wondering whether some other, smarter person couldn't have figured out a better resolution, or even avoided the conflict altogether. It wasn't until Monday night that it occurred to me: my best friend was back from vacation and I could call her. Although I was in the middle of cooking dinner, I didn't even wait to take the skillet off the stove. I just grabbed the phone and dialed.

We didn't have that much time. Dinner had to be served at my house, while at hers there were errands to run and kids' problems to solve before running out to a meeting at church. But for twenty minutes we talked while fielding interruptions or ignoring them, each telling her story and listening sympathetically to the other's. By the end we were laughing, perhaps just a little hysterically, as we compared notes about just how bad ordinary domestic drama can get. I can't remember which of us won the contest for having had the worst week. I do remember the intense relief that came just from talking to someone who didn't need explanations (she had known all the characters in my scene for years, as I had known hers, and we knew everybody's lines), someone who was unequivocally on my side but could still listen to something I had done and say bluntly, "Well, I'll bet that didn't help." It was like finding bread in a famine.

This unremarkable story will be instantly recognizable to everyone who has or ever had a best friend, that priceless combination of companion, comforter, and loving critic with whom everything can be shared unedited. But it also brings into view a few of the aspects of friendship I want to talk about: the things that make it a delight but at the same time takes effort to sustain; a relationship that calls forth deep loyalty but remains liable to loss even when all our intentions are good.

It is not entirely an accident that the friend I called is a woman, a mother of three who works outside the home, or that she is within a few years of my own age. Part of the foundation for friendship is a degree of likeness of one sort or another. The likeness may not include (as in this case) age, gender, and family situation, although because we tend to spend more time around those whose circumstances are similar to ours it often does. Still, if I were to explain what makes this woman my closest friend, I would not name any of those things, and some of my very close friends share few or none of those characteristics with me. The things that bind us to our friends are more than these. There must be something that makes us see the friend as like us in ways that are important, even central, to who we are. One of the deepest springs of friendship is the flash of something that feels like recognition: "There you are! You see what I'm saying! You will understand!"

As we observed in an earlier chapter, this means that not just anyone can be made a friend, at least not in any sense beyond the most casual. We choose our friends initially on the basis of some characteristic that we find attractive or enjoyable. Over time the friendship grows and deepens, or it contracts and withers, on the basis of the qualities we see in one another and the quality of our interaction with one another. Friendship, like romance, is what ethicists call a *preferential love*. That means it is selective and depends on the particular character and personality of the friend. It cannot be summoned as a matter of will, or owed to someone as a matter of duty. From that character of being given freely come both the unique gifts offered by friendship, and its vulnerability.

There is nothing quite like the discovery that someone we simply like also likes us, wants to spend time with us, and cares about us even though she or he does not have to. Part of the power of friendship is the knowledge that the friend is not stuck with us like our families are or obliged to assist us like the teachers and doctors and constant stream of others who take care of us and help us because it is somehow their responsibility to do so. Friends are there for us because they want to be.

The pleasure of being loved and chosen as a friend is distinct even from the mutual choosing and delight of lovers, for in romantic love we find both choice and need, and the free choice that begins romance is quickly joined to commitments that support but also constrain love. Friendship offers a unique degree of freedom, because unlike marriage it is not hedged about with promises and it does not fulfill a basic social need like child-rearing. Among all our relationships, this is the one that exists most purely for its own sake. A friendship that is sustained continues to seem remarkable, a gift that one cannot possibly deserve.

But it is by all the same tokens that friendship remains vulnerable. Because it *does* exist for its own sake, its survival depends entirely on the quality of the relationship: there is no other structure to support and maintain it. It can be starved by a lack of time, dissipated by distance and silence, or crowded out by other commitments and other relationships. Most threatening of all, and least in our control, friendship may be made impossible by the forces that continue to shape us into the people we are becoming. The things we once had in common may change or lose their importance in our lives. The very characteristics that once bound us together and made us confident of being understood may become barriers instead, as one person leaves an interest or a stage of life behind. When that happens, both may feel the loss, but feel powerless to prevent it.

As one observer has put it, what we naturally want is faithful friendships, relationships both completely free and completely reliable. It is not clear whether we can have them.[1] Because we human beings live in time and space, we are limited by circumstance and are liable to change, and our friendships rise and fall with tides we can only partly control. They can be carried away, as it seems, against our will. Is there anything besides good fortune that can help keep our friendships alive?

TIME AND DISTANCE

In an earlier chapter I recalled Aristotle's comment that friends have to eat a pound of salt together. He meant they have to spend so much time together that even something so incidental as the salt they share will add up to a substantial weight. In Aristotle's setting, this had the effect of making friendship one of the luxuries of upper-class males, because only they had leisure time and the freedom to use it as they would. Nevertheless, there is something to Aristotle's judgment: friendship takes time.

Most of us make our closest friends in the periods when we have the most time to devote to shared tasks and shared activities, and above all to shared conversation as we navigate our day-to-day existence. We make important friendships in childhood, in high school and college, and early in our adult lives. This is all before the demands of families and increasing work responsibilities make it hard to take the time regularly to review daily events with friends or to contemplate together unanswerable questions about the meaning of life into the small hours of the morning.

This is too simple a generalization, of course. I hope you are lucky enough to have encountered people who enrich and delight you in the middle of your life, and that you have had the good sense to cultivate deep and nourishing friendships with those people. I count it one of the great privileges of my life as a scholar that so much of my work consists of ongoing conversations with colleagues about things we both care about. It has given me a remarkable gift, providing the occasion for forming new friendships to cherish and celebrate long past the years of college and graduate school. But there are two things to note: first, it takes much more effort to nurture those adult friendships than it took when we were all nineteen and sharing a dorm hallway; second, because few of us are so lucky as to get to live with our friends, certain kinds of day-to-day intimacy are almost impossible to manage.

We no longer have the continual winding thread of conversation that characterizes the friendships of adolescence and early adulthood. There is less of the constant and incidental sharing of routine space and tasks as we interrupt each other's paper writing or trudge together to the laundromat when the socks really can't wait another day. Instead, we have discrete bits of time that must be planned, often carved out with some effort from a welter of other activities. We have to think about it in advance and coordinate our own schedules with those of our friends in order to be together at all. (It recently took me until August to schedule a birthday lunch with a friend who was born in June.) This takes a certain toll on spontaneity.

Also, if you are like me, you tend to wait to carve out time for your friends until they or you *need* it in one way or another, to deal with some challenge or recover from some blow or find respite when exhaustion threatens. (Witness my somewhat desperate call to my friend in the middle of making dinner.) Like families whose only reunions are at funerals, we meet in circumstances that don't exactly inspire playfulness or lightness of heart. They don't contribute much to balanced and healthy relationships either, because we always see each other in crisis mode.

But friendship loses something of its grace and freedom when we try to maintain it on a starvation diet or resort to it only in emergencies. Friends who do this are busy storing away nourishment when they are together, preparing for the long famine of being parent and spouse and worker and support system (you can fill in your own roles here). They are too pressed to be just regular people who get to enjoy their friends. It may be that our friendships are sturdy enough to survive this degree of neglect, and our friends sufficiently gracious to put up with it. (I thank God that so many of mine have been.) But we are a long way from honoring the ideas of our ancestors, who thought that friendship was a necessary part of a good and full human life— one of the things that *makes* us human, and even one of the tools God uses to make us holy.

So far I have been talking about the struggle to sustain friendships when the limit is just competition for our time. All of this is complicated even further by the fact that, to paraphrase an old Carole King song, nobody seems to stay in one place anymore. The friend I called at dinner time was hundreds of miles away and in a different time zone. I feel the distance especially keenly in her case, because there was a period of a few years when we lived across the driveway from one another and could holler out the window when we wanted something.

In those days, walking into each other's kitchens required no plan, no agenda, not even any clear idea of what one wanted beyond the seemingly natural presence of the other. I accuse my friend of deserting me because she moved away first, but in fact I have moved twice since then, and so has she. The richness of casual daily intimacy was something we both left behind with regret, but commitments to spouses and to the communities we each serve called us in different directions, and so we went.

It is possible that as a society our priorities are out of order and we might learn something from those forms of shared Christian life that vow stability (remaining permanently in one location) as a spiritual discipline. But those of us who are in service to a vocation or a community that has a claim on our presence, or who are married to someone who is, may in fact be called on to leave our dearest friends behind. We have to try to find a way not to leave behind the gifts and the fidelity of friendship as well.

There has been much discussion in recent years of the distinction between the quality of time shared and its quantity. This discussion has been carried on mostly in defense of the idea that an increase in the focus and quality of time spent could make up for having significantly less time to devote to a relationship overall. Much of this has been debated in relation to the hot-button issue of whether parents, particularly mothers, should work outside the home while children are young. (I will not venture into that debate, except to observe that the only reasonable answer seems to be, "It depends.")

My experience and the experience of those friends and acquaintances with whom I have discussed it over the years suggests that the claim that quality is more important than quantity is true in friendship—but only within limits. It matters a great deal what stage the relationship is in when time becomes limited. It matters too what kind of friendship one has in view. If the friendship is far advanced, based on years of constant close contact and deep personal sharing, it will almost certainly withstand prolonged absence and limited opportunities to be together. Those who have maintained such bonds over years often remark about the durability and the degree of intimacy these friendships are able to sustain. You will hear them speak of being able to pick up the phone after many months and resume a conversation as if after a brief interruption. But this does not mean that the change will not be painful or that it will not entail a real loss.

Friends who suffer such a change in circumstances should expect to go through a genuine experience of grief, having to mourn and let go of a kind of relationship that is no longer possible for them. For, inevitably, with distance the friendship *does* change its character. It loses the immediacy of sharing unprocessed experience, and the spontaneity of dropping in on impulse. The friends can no longer share their day-to-day lives as a matter of course. They lose the liberty of being able to take each other for granted in a certain benign sense, of being able simply to assume the other's presence.

The fact that time for the friendship has to be planned and deliberately taken means that the relationship becomes more reflective and more self-aware, but also more selective. Just "catching up" means turning the random events of many days, weeks, or months into something like a narrative. In the process, one chooses what to relate, sets apart things that seem important to share. This process already forces a degree of interpretation that both reveals and obscures our experience. It means that our friend now sees us through a kind of lens shaped by how we see ourselves.

As a result, distance makes it possible to hide, even to disappear, perhaps without quite realizing it. The genuineness of the connection can be eroded over time, becoming more and more superficial. We still call one another, and call one another friends, but we gradually replace the joys and challenges of real intimacy with newsy chats that stay safely near the surface. These are the oral equivalent of the Christmas card letters that many families send out; they are fine as far as they go, but everyone reading them recognizes that they are getting an edited version of the story.

This effect can be offset to some degree by long and intimate knowledge and the insight it continues to offer, as long as the friends are willing to share bad news as well as good, questions and perplexities as well as resolutions. An old friend may be able to listen on the phone for half an hour and know you are in trouble, often before you know it yourself. This can be powerfully life giving, even life saving.

Some six months after my father's death, in a long-distance phone call, I happened to mention to a dear and experienced friend something about how I was feeling—or more accurately, about how *little* I was feeling. The press of tasks to attend to surrounding the death, other family members to care for, and the immediate return to work afterward had left me little space or liberty to grieve. But my father's had been a slow and terrible death by inches that took years, and it left those of us who stood by numb and hollowed out with helpless waiting. Through all this and in the months afterward I was functioning just fine to all appearances—meeting my classes, caring for my family, fulfilling various professional obligations. Meanwhile, I hadn't given my growing sense of disconnection much thought.

But the friend who knew me so well asked a few questions and quickly realized that I was sliding toward depression, and was perhaps not too far from being in danger. It was her insight and her cheerful but firm direction ("Okay, sweetheart, here is what you're going to do now") that got me to notice what I would certainly have recognized in someone else. She walked with me through the steps that gave me room both to mourn and to heal. I do not know how long it would have taken me otherwise. I am not even certain that I would have realized what was happening before the depression that was then just taking a grip had become firmly entrenched and dangerous.

But the difficulty of sustaining friendship at a distance, when the constraints of time are particularly severe, is not purely bad news. It can offer gifts of its own because it forces us to pay attention to the friendship as something that needs sustenance. It requires taking time to attend exclusively to this friend, traveling to visit or arranging to meet somewhere, and that requirement alone invests our time together with importance and memorability. We discover the dearness of each particular friend partly in the ongoing deprivation of being far away. It is this discovery that continually renews the gratitude and presence to one another that keeps the friendship alive. Suddenly the language of the ancients about a friend as the other half of oneself, and their talk about the longing to be with the friend who is absent, does not seem so strange.

DEVELOPMENT AND CHANGE

Because friendship does not simply arise from our circumstances like family affection and is not aimed at the construction of a unique bond between the participants as in romantic love, it very often has what might be called a third point or a focus. Two people are involved, but there is also an other, third thing that the friendship grows up around: an activity or an interest or a task that indicates what the friendship is about. (A whole group of friends may in fact be gathered together in this way, but for simplicity's sake I speak here only of two.)

When we are very young, the third point may be just the developmental task that occupies us at the time: navigating fifth grade, finding a way to survive as the youngest in the family, or whatever challenge presents itself. In later adolescence and adulthood, when the choices and challenges that confront us are more complicated and more diverse, friendships still form around some interest or project. But now the array of those possible meeting points is very wide, and in negotiating them we are engaged in the delicate dance between discovering who we are and choosing who we will become.

Friendships emerge with those who share some aspect of the self we are at once finding and constructing, and they serve both to confirm and to shape that self. This is why our closest friends so often share some basic commitment with us: the centrality of a role like parent or spouse, a profession to which we are devoted, a pursuit or a project we are passionate about, or a social or religious ideal that we hold dear. All this is a way of saying again what Aristotle observed 2,500 years ago: that our most important friendships are grounded in our character. They reflect the person we are and want to be, the things we delight in and hope for and care about deeply.

Earlier I suggested that because our deepest friendships are based on features of who we are, they remain vulnerable to the changes that can occur in people over time. I was not speaking purely theoretically. I made my first important friend when I was twelve, and lost her for good when I was twenty-six. Nothing happened to her; in fact, for many years as adults we lived a half-hour's drive apart. We just ended up lost to each other, so it was less painful to lapse into silence than to confront the fact that we could no longer be friends in any sense that mattered to us. We had been too close for too many formative years to settle for something entirely superficial, and we loved each other too well to spend our time trying to change each other.

Now, some decades later, it seems to me that I could have managed the end better but on the whole the loss was inevitable. We just became people who no longer prized the same things, who could not honestly share or support each other's vision of what was worth doing or who it was worthwhile to be. From my point of view, the friend I knew and loved disappeared sometime in college, taken up into a world of fraternity parties and football games, occupied by a circle of friends and interests I could not share or understand. From her standpoint, I imagine I too became someone else: someone too serious, too judgmental, with too little openness and too little sympathy for the things she enjoyed and the goals she was choosing for herself.

In retrospect, I am sure I was clumsy and insensitive. I was arrogant enough at the time to think I knew better than she who she really was, and I betrayed my dismay and disapproval as she chose a life that seemed to me beneath her intelligence and sensitivity. But I doubt that greater humility and reticence on my part would have done anything but delay the result. By the time we were young adults beginning to make lives for ourselves, the disparity between the things each of us sought and the things each of us cared about was too great for anything beyond a dogged loyalty. We managed that much for some years, and then she cut the ties, simply not responding to calls. It was, I think, not indifference but a way of honoring what we had meant to each other by refusing to let it deteriorate any further.

Losses like this are painful, and I have thought a lot since then about how they could be prevented. Even now it does not seem to me that they can. Of course one could decide not to take the risk of forming important friendships at all, but that is like choosing to starve oneself to death to avoid the possibility of famine. It is also true that changes in character are more likely as a result of the developmental changes of coming to maturity, so friendships formed in adolescence are especially vulnerable to this kind of disintegration. At the same time, such friendships are themselves formative, part of how we try on alternative versions of who we want to become. Avoiding them is avoiding some of the work of growing up, risks and all.

Besides, it's not clear that the strategy of waiting until we are grown to make real investments in friendship would work to keep us safe from loss. Although character in adults is relatively stable, and we thus have a well-founded sense of knowing who people are and what they are likely to do, it is never wholly fixed. Even full-fledged adults can and do change, for good or for ill. They can undergo conversions of one sort or another, finding a life's passion or abandoning it, coming to faith or losing it, being battered by suffering or raised to real nobility by it. They can be moved toward compassion or hardened into cynicism by their experience. We are always in the process of becoming who we are to be, and there is always a chance that changes will take us or those we love past the reach of our friendships, to places where their understanding and intimacy cannot extend.

Early in this chapter I asked whether there was anything other than good luck that could help us keep our friendships alive. I have talked a little about the possibilities of sustaining friendships with limited time and across distance. But we have yet to talk about what strategies there are for maintaining our friendships through the changes that time and experience impose on all of us. Acknowledging that there can be no guarantees, still it is a question worth asking: What might enable us to be faithful in friendship?

STRATEGIES FOR WEATHERING STORMS

We start with the challenges. Significant changes in life situations do not in themselves force changes in character, but they can bring out new and unfamiliar aspects of someone's personality. This is often to the good, such as when we discover a tender and nurturing side to the old friend who suddenly has stepchildren to raise, or meet unexpected resources of skill and administrative competence in the friend who returns to work after her children start school. Here friendship is just a matter of honoring and celebrating what we see emerging in the person we know and love. It means taking time to *pay attention* and incorporate this new feature into our picture of the friend and into the time we spend together.

But sometimes the life changes are difficult and unwelcome, and they place aspects of character under tremendous pressure. Perhaps, like me, you have had friends who, devastated by divorce, were consumed by anger and bitterness even years afterward. Sometimes people, bent on the assignment of blame, seem unable to get beyond a continual rehashing of the conflict. The only aspect of friendship they show any interest in is having a partisan, someone to confirm that their view is entirely right and that their estranged spouse is wholly the villain. It is not only hard to be around someone frozen in that place but also hard to know how to act as a friend when what is asked for seems so clearly to be of no real benefit to the person we care about.

The insight provided by long knowledge may help by offering a perspective from which to understand how a friend is responding. For instance, a man I knew who reacted very badly to his wife's departure was easier to understand and bear with if you knew that his mother had abandoned him when he was a young boy. We may try over time to call a person stuck in such a place to a renewed engagement with the future. Sometimes our history together provides an opening to remind our friend of other commitments and other possibilities, of a broader horizon within which to find peace and the resources for recovery. For a time an old friend may be able to serve as the bearer of memory and of hope.

Friends may be changed by other griefs as well—deeply shaken by the loss of a job, the death of a partner, or the final collapse of some long-held aspiration. Such times can place a strain on friendship, as the pain of loss may be expressed in jealousy or withdrawal or hostility. Often the challenge is just that there seems to be so little one can do, and the burden of standing by suffering we cannot remedy is hard for many of us to bear. It may be tempting to withdraw because we feel useless and inadequate. But walking with someone through dark and difficult times is a basic part of friendship, the work of which includes allowing grief time to come to peace. If the loss is profound enough, the process may take some years. Still, the gift of presence is the most important and often the hardest one to give, and it may mean far more to those who are grieving than we can imagine.

Years ago, a brand new seminary graduate had been in his first parish assignment for all of two weeks when he got a terrible call. The father of a young family in his congregation had accidentally struck and killed his two-year-old son while backing out of the driveway that morning. Not knowing what else to do, the young minister went to the couple's home, where he found them sitting frozen in shock and horror. He tried to speak, to do what he thought a minister should and find some words of comfort or faith to help. He found that he was too overcome to do anything more than weep helplessly with the devastated parents. Somehow the family and the church got through the days of the wake and the funeral, and one day months later the young pastor tried to express to the parents his great regret that he had been unable to offer them help in their time of overwhelming loss. They would not hear of his apology, for they insisted that he had offered them the one essential thing by staying with them in those hours when nothing but tears would come.[2]

But if friends are those who refuse to abandon us when we are in trouble, where and how we offer our support may still be a matter of careful judgment. One aspect of the care we owe to friends is the need to be deeply aware of the ways in which changes in our situation or in theirs may create new risks and new issues for the friendship itself. Since the release of the popular movie *When Harry Met Sally,* it has become practically a party game to entertain the question, Can men and women genuinely be friends, or as the protagonist puts it, does sex always get in the way?

Of course many times it is not a problem for what begins as a friendship to take on the added dimensions of a romance, and many marriages are richer for having a history grounded in friendship. But the situation is different when one or both of the friends is married or has a vow of singleness and celibacy to keep. My experience and that of the many colleagues with whom I have discussed the matter suggests that men and women with other commitments *can* be friends, even friends of real and sustained closeness. But it requires both practiced self-awareness and careful consideration for each other's vulnerabilities.

Friends both of whom are secure and content in marriages of their own may have the easiest time with this, but even for them it is a mistake to imagine that the trust, liking, and mutual enjoyment of friendship can never shade over into overt sexual attraction. Also, periods of friction and relative distance are an ordinary part of marriage. These may create temporary alienation, frustration, and loneliness that present risks for the married partner who maintains close friendships with people of the opposite sex. For friends whose situations offer even less protection, vigilance is needed. It is crucial that we pay careful and honest attention both to our own and to our friend's real situation. We have to think hard about how we can genuinely and truthfully be present to and cherish this friend, doing good and not harm to the person we love.

These day-to-day challenges are apart from the more profound risks created by deep and long-lasting estrangement in a marriage. If we find ourselves in such circumstances, it may be very difficult to remain in emotionally intimate friendships with those to whom we might become seriously attracted. Equally, the situations of our friends must be part of our concern. When we or our friends are particularly vulnerable, we must be very careful about where and how we live out our friendship. We may find it necessary to limit the time we spend together, replacing face-to-face conversation with correspondence and telephone calls, or enjoying our time together in groups with other friends. It is a balance of some delicacy, of finding ways to stand close to our friend when one of us is in trouble, without letting our friendship itself become part of a new crisis.

CHANGES IN CHARACTER

So far I have spoken chiefly of difficulties that affect our friendships from the outside: when circumstances keep us apart and threaten to erode our connection to each other, or when some crisis faced by one of the friends places him or her under great pressure. These put various kinds of strain on the relationship and may, for a time at least, make it hard to know how to love this friend. But now it is time to address what are in many ways the most difficult challenges to friendship, or at least the ones about which the least can be done. These are the actual changes in character that come about because of an underlying shift in values and beliefs, so that the person in some measure becomes some-one else. These can sometimes be prompted by one of the crises we have named, but it is the resulting change in character and conviction that creates the more serious problem.

What are we to do when a friend seems to be changing or disappearing before our eyes, when we feel like the person we know has gone and left behind a stranger? The first answer, and usually the hardest to live out, is once more to wait. Here again this means more than marking time, waiting for our friend to come back to us as the person he or she was. It calls for a more active and attentive presence, one with the humility to be ready to learn a new thing not only about our friend but even possibly about ourselves.

Such waiting takes patience and flexibility, and like the wait-ing needed by a marriage in trouble, it may mean a season of deprivation, when the needs and desires normally fulfilled by the relationship must be let go unanswered. It is in some ways easier and in other ways harder than the corresponding challenge within a marriage. On the one hand, few of us depend as heav-ily on any single friendship to meet basic emotional needs as we depend on our spouses. On the other hand, because we depend less on this relationship, it is also easier to withdraw as the friend has seemed to, turning to other people and other friendships and shutting the door behind you.

If we are to try to remain constant as a friend through changes that threaten to take this person far from us, it is necessary to put aside whatever we may feel of hurt and anger, our sense of grief and impending loss. Indeed, as far as possible we have to put our-selves altogether to one side and try to pay attention to our friend and what is happening to her or him. We have to be willing to wait in openness and hope for a person with whom we can remain connected, even if the nature of that connection is changed. And when all is done, it may not be enough.

The philosopher and theologian Søren Kierkegaard gives us an image for this kind of waiting in hope for a return that may not come. He imagines a couple on a dance floor, moving and turning gracefully and in unison. Suddenly one of them leaves the floor abruptly, abandoning the dance and the partner. In Kierkegaard's image, the abandoned dancer simply waits, remaining in the posture of the dance, ready to receive and embrace the partner should he or she return, so that the dance can go on.

The image is lovely but also sad, because the completion of the dance may never be. Friends really can undergo changes that may make them into people we can no longer deeply share our life with or even no longer trust. And of course over time we may change as well. It may simply not be possible to have the special relationship we call friendship with the person this friend has become, or to remain friends with someone when we ourselves have undergone a basic change in commitments.

What remains in this case is a debt of gratitude and loyalty for the sake of the friendship that once was. This may sometimes be expressed in the maintenance of some degree of contact and a readiness to offer help if it is needed. In other cases it may be only a matter of well-wishing, and the sort of hope that theologians call *eschatological:* the hope that in some restored and finally fulfilled creation God may enable the love of friendship to bind all people into one.

FRIENDSHIP AND HOLINESS

I touched briefly in an earlier chapter on spiritual friendship. This was how the classical idea of *virtue friendship* was reshaped in light of Christian ideals of shared growth in holiness. In spiritual friendship, the "third thing" the friendship is about is growing in the love of God and neighbor. The modern tendency is to suppose that this spiritual focus must somehow dilute the friendship, as if it could not truly be a matter of genuine personal love and intimacy between the partners because it points toward God. Those who first developed this tradition, and those who still claim it today, insist that the spiritual dimension *intensifies* the human friendship.

Now, it is true that through the love of the spiritual friend one comes to see and love God better, and through it as well one becomes better able to see and love the neighbors one encounters as strangers or even enemies. So the particular love for such a friend is not a substitute for neighbor love but a school for it. But it is equally true that, being oriented toward the Creator who is also the Author of all love, such friends see each other more clearly, more completely, more truly. Their love for each other is made deeper and more enduring because they see and cherish each other for who they really are, and they are joined by what is nearest their hearts. So the love of neighbor does not substitute for friendship either; instead, neighbor love *grows out of* friendship, binding the friends more closely as friends in its pursuit.

It is a mistake to suppose that spiritual friendship is a path for special people: those who are especially pious or somehow spiritually gifted, or those who aspire to sainthood. The practice of spiritual friendship reflects more about the nature of the goal than it does about the individual participants. Those who want to grow and be nurtured in love seek out other people because, it turns out, we learn to love in relationships and come to see ourselves and our growing edges more readily through others' eyes than through our own.

It is also a misunderstanding to imagine that those united in spiritual friendship spend all their time together in church, in meditation, or engaged in serious and pious pursuits like studying the Bible. In general, the things that spiritual friends do together are a great deal like the things any good friends do. They spend time together. They talk and laugh and share their lives, their triumphs and challenges, their heartaches and the things they worry about. They play and relax and enjoy each other's company. And they help when there is trouble or need. But spiritual friends also ask each other difficult and uncomfortable questions, and tell one another the truth even when it is hard. Most distinctively, they pray together, and in an archaic phrase that nevertheless conveys something central to this relationship, they "keep watch over each other's souls."[3]

For spiritual friendship, for all its joys, is not only about the pleasures of deep human connection, sweet as these are. As strong a support as it offers, it is not only about support either. It is about holding one another up, but also about holding each other accountable, in gentleness and humility, for the steady pursuit of a goal that remains always ahead: simply to love God with all your heart and soul and mind and strength, and your neighbor as yourself. This means that spiritual friendship involves hearing the news, both good and bad, of a lifelong journey on which most of us take many wrong turns. It calls sometimes for offering comfort, sometimes for encouragement, sometimes for reproach. At other times it means the declaration of forgiveness announced in Christ's name to one who needs to hear it spoken out loud. At all times it calls for attention and discernment, and the constant prayer to say and do what is needed.

This is a work of long patience and one that takes a surprising amount of courage. There is no use lying in prayer, but telling the truth—all of it!—in the presence of those whose respect you would like to keep is nothing short of scalding sometimes. It is no easier being on the other side either. Hearing the secrets of others' souls can be painful, even terrifying. One feels the weight, however briefly, before handing it to the One who bears all secrets and all sins.

But for those who sustain such friendships, their fruit is great. We practice the life we aim at together and receive strength and help to continue. And at times we lean on the faith and hope of our friends when our own is exhausted and we cannot even find our way to prayer.

LOVING YOUR FRIENDS IN GOD

Augustine was the first Christian writer in the West to talk extensively about friendship and spiritual life. Because his writing is so vividly personal, he gives us a window into what it might mean to love friends "in God" through one of the stories he tells about his life. Since it comes early in his autobiography, long before his coming to faith, it is in part a tale of the corrupting power of friendship and its capacity to lead us astray. But it calls forth his deepest and most eloquent reflection on the friendship of those whose love is centered in God.[4]

When Augustine was a young man of twenty-one, he returned from schooling in Carthage to teach in his hometown of Thagaste. His closest and most constant companion was another young scholar whom he had known as a boy. For that whole year they were inseparable, and the brilliant and charismatic Augustine brought his friend under the influence of a Gnostic sect that attracted him, the Manicheans. In this way both were drawn away from the Catholic faith of their families and, as Augustine would later see it, entangled in lies and ensnared by pride. (It is in this connection that Augustine calls his love for his friends "friendship all unfriendly."[5])

Augustine's friend fell ill with a fever, and Augustine tells of sitting anxiously by his side when his illness was so grave that it was expected he might die. During this time the parents of the young man had him baptized. (This was a common pattern for Christians in this period, who feared to commit any sin after baptism and so often delayed it until death approached.) Augustine thought little of this at the time, expecting his friend to laugh it off when he recovered. In fact, the friend did rally, and when he could talk Augustine said something jesting about his baptism, expecting him to join in despising the rite as mere bodily superstition. But the friend shocked Augustine by looking at him like an enemy and threatening to send him away if he persisted in making light of the sacrament. Augustine was dismayed, but he wrote it off to the lingering effects of fever.

Augustine went home that night expecting to return to keep his friend company through his convalescence. But unexpectedly the young man took a turn for the worse and died a few days later. Augustine was undone. He writes, "My heart was utterly darkened by sorrow, and everywhere I looked I saw only death."[6] He was able to enjoy nothing, and for months, he says, "only tears were sweet to me."[7] He wandered the town, "hating all places because he was not in them,"[8] until at length he fled back to Carthage, thinking he would miss his friend less in places they had never been together. It was in fact many months before time and the distraction of work began to bring about some healing, and Augustine was able to engage in living once more.

All this is what Augustine experienced at the time. When he recounts the story in the *Confessions* he is looking back across twenty-five years, from the vantage point of the conversion that had brought his passionate and restless spirit to peace. Now he praises the mercy of God in what seemed a tragedy, for by it God had rescued the young man he loved from Augustine's dangerous influence and brought him safely home. Therefore Augustine may hope to meet him again, in a realm where death no longer holds sway. But even this is not the great lesson he takes from the story.

Recalling the bitter loss of his friend launches Augustine into an extended reflection on the nature of our loves for all things that pass away. The power of his writing, and what has given him such a profound influence on Christian thought, is that he is able to write of all these things with a full and eloquent appreciation for the loveliness and goodness they do have. But, he says, we both dishonor God and also betray what we mean as love when we fail to see these transient and mortal things for what they are.

Their beauty and goodness, indeed their very being, spring from the reality of God, who makes and sustains them from moment to moment. But it is their nature to come to an end. We use and enjoy them well when we see in them the gift of the Creator, the image of God's vitality and beauty, and turn our gratitude and praise to God. But they become snares to us when we love them *instead of* God, or when we cleave to them as if in themselves they could bear the weight of our longing, which is always for eternity. Love for creatures must be referred back to their Source, or else "they rend the soul with pestilential desires, because she longs to rest secure in the created things she loves. But in these things there is no resting place to be found."[9]

This reservation applies to the physical objects we might love, but in a different way it applies to the persons we love as well: to be loved rightly, they must be loved in relation to God. "If souls please you, let them be loved in God, for in themselves they are changeable, but in Him firmly established."[10] Augustine takes his own utter despair at his friend's death as a sign that he did not in fact love his friend well. Not only did he lead him into a false religion, but there was so little truth in Augustine's understanding of the nature of a human being that he loved a phantasm, loved his own delight in his friend rather than the friend as he truly was: a man whose only abiding life was in God. It was Augustine's own false understanding that plunged him into darkness: "For why had that first sorrow so easily penetrated to the quick except that I had poured out my soul into the dust, by loving a man as if he would never die...?"[11]

The conclusion he offers is this: "Blessed is he who loves thee, and loves his friend in thee, and his enemy for thy sake; for he alone loses none dear to him, if all are dear in Him who cannot be lost."[12] Friends who love one another in God certainly are not preserved from grief or from the longing for those from whom they are separated. But they are kept from complete despair. They will not, as Paul puts it, grieve "as those who have no hope" (1 Thess. 4:13).

Love Without Boundaries:
Strangers and Enemies

The image was completely arresting. As many times as I had seen it, it still always stopped me short and made me wonder: Who is she? What is she thinking behind that gaze at once guarded and challenging? What has she seen? *And what ever became of her?* Evidently I am not the only one. The photograph was on the cover of *National Geographic's* 2002 collection called *The 100 Best Pictures,* culled from the literally millions of photos archived in the magazine's 113 years of publication. It was chosen for the cover because it had drawn more letters than any other photograph in *National Geographic's* history. It was the face of a young Afghan girl, perhaps twelve or thirteen, photographed in a refugee camp in 1984. Even the photographer could not get her out of his mind. He made many attempts to find her in subsequent years, and in 2002 finally located her, by then a grown woman with daughters of her own, living near the border with Pakistan.[1]

In the eighteen years it took to track down the subject and give her a name, not a week went by in which someone did not write to the magazine asking for information about the girl. Some people wrote offering to adopt her, and many others wanted to help with her support and education. Partly this is testimony to the power a single photograph can have, summing up in one image a whole vast complex of events and emotions or capturing a long-running catastrophe like a war in a single instant. Dozens of such images are familiar around the globe: icons for whole generations of a time, a place, or an event.

But the response to the picture is also an indication of something important about how human beings are wired, so to speak. It shows the way our imaginations and our emotions are keyed to respond to what is *particular*. It is not just the beauty of the child that stops us, although she is in fact strikingly beautiful. It is the powerful sense of the *reality* of this one, individual girl: a single piece of flotsam caught in the torrent of the Soviet-Afghan conflict, intensely alive and achingly vulnerable, staring out at us from the flap of a tent half a world away. It makes us want to keep her safe.

MOVING FROM STRANGERS
TO NEIGHBORS

The capacity to be moved to active compassion by the face of a stranger, and the impulse to help that comes from that compassion, is deeply rooted in human beings. It is one of the best things about us. Of course there were thousands upon thousands of children in the refugee camps spawned by the decades-long struggle for dominance in Afghanistan, just as there were thousands of others in Africa, in Palestine, and elsewhere around the world. There was no difficulty in finding them. Everyone viewing the photograph knew that, and the photographer who took the picture had seen it for himself. Yet their compassion went out to this single unnamed child, and so did their offers of help.[2] Why is that?

This is a phenomenon well known to social scientists. It is also known to the directors of charitable organizations, and to those who do their fundraising. There is even a special term for it: it is the difference between *identified lives* and *statistical lives*. Everyone knew about the thousands of children in those camps, but they were only numbers. Numbers alone do not touch us, do not wound our consciences or pierce our hearts. The photograph, though only an image, was so powerful and so effective because it gave the viewer a sense of encountering *this child*. She was a particular, identifiable *someone* caught in terrible circumstances, and that was enough to make thousands of strangers reach out to try to help her.

What is it that moves another human being in trouble from the category of stranger into the category of one whom we may see as a neighbor? What supports our ability to identify and empathize, to care and take the risks of caring for someone to whom we have no other connection than our common humanity? Along with being moved by an identifiable individual, we are also more likely to respond with action to needs on a scale we can comprehend. As impressive as we find the panoramic images of devastation after some natural disaster or the statistics about the dead, the missing, and the displaced that are the steady drumbeat of newscasts, suffering of that magnitude quickly exceeds our grasp. It leaves us numb.

The gift and limitation of today's global mass media is precisely this: it instantly takes us anywhere and everywhere on a planet a large proportion of whose six and a half *billion* inhabitants are suffering under some kind of hardship. We can see the drought and famine in sub-Saharan Africa, witness the thousands fleeing genocide in the Sudan, and watch the slow excavation of whole villages buried by a mudslide in Central America. We can see but we cannot really get our minds around it all.

We may be told, for instance, that twenty-four thousand people die every day of the effects of malnutrition.[3] We may even anguish over the fact. But the enormity of it staggers the imagination, and that in itself is paralyzing. We cannot begin to conceive of a response that answers such a disaster, and in the face of that incapacity it is hard not to despair and simply avert our gaze. Sometimes, the combination of helplessness and guilt even makes us resent those whose suffering we feel unable to address.

Much more reliable are our responses to a situation we can at least imagine, in a world we know or can be brought to feel we know. This accounts for the practices of charities, which so often begin fundraising appeals with the story of a single village or a single family vividly told: "Here is what a flock of chickens could mean to this farming community." They offer sponsorships to connect donors with an individual family, or they show a bright and heartening shot of a smiling child in front of a newly refurbished school. The message in each case is the same: "Something needs to be done, and here is something you can do right now. Supply these needs, sponsor this family, support this project, and you can make a difference." This plea appeals to our awakened sympathy and our compassion, but it also responds to our powerful need for a sense of agency: a belief in our capacity to do something about suffering, the true scale of which we cannot take in, cannot even imagine. It is this belief that enables us to open ourselves to caring.

BARRIERS TO COMPASSION

But just as some things aid us in recognizing other human beings as neighbors, help us to respond with the active compassion that is the hallmark of neighbor love, other things make it more difficult to do so. One of these deterrents is just getting tired. No matter how we encounter the pressing needs of strangers, there seems to be a limit to how long we can remain open and responsive to them.

In the aftermath of the attacks of September 11, 2001, contributions to the American Red Cross and other relief agencies responding to the needs of victims and their families came in at a rate never seen before. So rapid and overwhelming was the reaction that systems for tracking and directing funds and other resources were swamped and it took many months to untangle the resulting confusion. Likewise, when Hurricane Katrina struck the Gulf Coast of the United States in late August 2005, there was a huge outpouring of public support. Donations of every imaginable kind flowed in, and volunteers traveled from all over the country to help with rescue and relocation, cleanup and rebuilding.

But in the previous winter the country had been jolted out of its mood of postholiday celebration by news and images of an enormous, earthquake-born tsunami that struck Southeast Asia the day after Christmas 2004. In some places it simply carried away whole communities; in others it left random patterns of destruction, washing one house with its inhabitants out to sea and leaving another standing. The geographical scope of the disaster was unprecedented, and the logistical challenges of responding to communities whose fragile infrastructure was simply gone were staggering.

Although worldwide humanitarian response was rapid and significant, experts in disaster relief and the leaders of philanthropic organizations talked about a dampening of U.S. response. This was seen both at the level of official government aid and in private donations. The decline was attributed to something the experts called *compassion fatigue*. It was not so much that Americans' material resources were exhausted. It was rather that their capacity to identify with and reach out to suffering strangers had been depleted. The psychological burden of empathy for the victims of one more tragedy, especially one of such unthinkable proportions and so far from home, was too great for many people.

But our limited compassion, our finite capacity to embrace one another as fellow sufferers when crises occur, is not the only problem. The daily conditions of modern life, its scale and complexity, also create barriers to seeing one another as neighbors. As our globe becomes increasingly urbanized and interconnected, the proximity of so many people and the flood of so much information cause many of us to withdraw in some measure. This may be no more than a reaction to overstimulation, to the need for solitude or at least for a social world of a more manageable size. Increasingly we act to insulate ourselves from others we do not know, thus ensuring that they will remain only strangers to us.

We walk down the street talking on cell phones rather than being attentive to the people we pass on the sidewalk, and we ride on the subway plugged into earphones or hidden behind a newspaper rather than talking to those sitting next to us. This creates for us an island of aloneness in the middle of a crowd, and increasingly we avoid being with others altogether. We trade social events like going to a concert or to the theater for private entertainment, listening to music on sophisticated home stereo systems or watching rented DVD's on our own large-screen televisions. The globe is often said to be shrinking, and it seems that many of us are feeling crowded.

It is easy to exaggerate the importance of behavior like this, to take it as more indicative of basic character than it really is. For example, city people are frequently thought of as cold and unfriendly by people accustomed to rural communities, simply because their habits of public behavior are more aloof. (Ironically, American city dwellers traveling in many European capitals report the inhabitants to be rude and hostile for the same reason. Compared to Muscovites, it seems, New Yorkers are positively chatty.) In reality, such habits are often just strategies for negotiating daily life under pressure, when one's immediate neighbors number in the hundreds of thousands and living conditions are stressful. But they do add one more hurdle to be overcome if we are really to come to see as neighbors those whom we confront as strangers, and to extend our care to include them.

A last barrier to recognizing one another as neighbors is difference—all the distinctions of language, culture, ethnic heritage, and national identity that mark out human beings as members of diverse communities. Such human differences have always existed, of course, and have always had the capacity to divide. To take a preeminent American example, our deeply stained national history means that the category of race retains much of its power to divide us, despite being recognized today as a social distinction with no genetic basis. Race may be a biological fiction, but it remains a potent fiction all the same.

What is new is that in an era of global travel and trade, of widespread migration and the dislocations caused by war, political instability, and economic hardship, we are likely to encounter more of such differences. And we are likely to do so more constantly, closer to home, and across more dimensions than in any previous generation. Unlike the millions of overwhelmingly European descent who poured through Ellis Island in the late nineteenth and early twentieth centuries, many recent immigrants bear visible and permanent signs of difference such as distinctive skin tone and facial features. In addition, some of them have entered the country without legal documentation, fleeing crippling unemployment, desperate poverty, or political oppression and violence at home. These visible differences and the issues of legal status add greatly to the anxiety and isolation that newcomers face, particularly in our post–9/11 atmosphere of increased suspicion toward foreigners.

That suspicion is something even legal residents feel keenly and personally. In early 2004, when the U.S. invasions of Afghanistan and Iraq were still front-page news every day, I crossed the street to welcome neighbors who had just moved in. The father of the family came forward with formal politeness to shake my hand. He introduced himself and each of his children by name, adding, "We are from Afghanistan, but we are not terrorists." A climate in which someone feels a need to say that is one in which the barriers that divide us and keep us from seeing the stranger as a neighbor whom one is called upon to love are dauntingly high.

FINDING OUR WAY BACK

It is not hard, then, to identify the things that stand in the way of our recognizing one another as neighbors or even being willing to do so. There are the psychological hurdles of anonymity, the scale of human suffering we are aware of, and the paralysis that comes from feeling helpless. There are also barriers as basic as fatigue and the continual overstimulation of urban life, challenges as permanent as human differences, and the sense of the unknown other as a threat. How can we find our way to recognition and care without being overwhelmed and driven to despair or frightened into retreat and self-protection? How do we grow in our ability to hear and respond to the second commandment that Jesus called so like the first: that we are to love our neighbors as ourselves?

The first thing to say is that we should expect any such growth to take a while. The readiness to show compassion to the stranger, not just impulsively or occasionally but steadily and reliably, will be the fruit of a long process of being shaped over time and in a community. Like any art that engages the whole person, the capacity to recognize the stranger as our neighbor will require learning and change. We will need to practice it, and it will require discipline.

But the fact that love of the neighbor whom we do not know takes work doesn't mean it is not authentic. We mustn't suppose that something is not really love because it does not simply well up in us spontaneously. As we have seen, even the natural loves that bind us to parents and children, spouses and friends, often take work and are learned as well as called forth spontaneously.

And even though this form of love extends beyond what is natural in some ways, none of us begins to learn it altogether from scratch. We are equipped to empathize and identify with one another by our earliest and most basic impulses. We are joined by the things that make infants smile in response to smiles, even on unfamiliar faces, and by those that make grown-ups wince and recoil at the sight of any human being's suffering. In some fundamental way we are designed to "feel with" one another.

Beyond that, with the exception of those who have been victims of the most extreme neglect or abuse, the raw material of our natural connections to one another has been a thousand times reinforced by our actual social experience. We have been in some measure prepared for the love of neighbor by every relationship of care and trust we have ever had, by every simple courtesy exchanged on the street, and by every act of kindness that has been extended to us over our lives. But because there really *are* obstacles, opposing forces that lead us to keep our distance from others and to close ourselves off from care and compassion, it will take more than this. Neither nature nor ordinary social life will lead us to the expansive and consistent embrace of the stranger as neighbor that is the capstone of Christian moral life.

Much of the foundation for the practice of loving strangers as neighbors comes from the distinctive story Christians tell and from the particular convictions they share. We are all accustomed to language about "the human community," and the idea that all humanity forms a single family is one we hear in speeches on occasions like United Nations Day. Language like this can touch and inspire any of us, and it has been invoked masterfully by public figures such as Martin Luther King Jr. to call a whole nation to moral responsibility. But it has a different force and credibility for those who believe that all human beings are the creatures of one God, a God who cares for and yearns after them like a parent, no matter what their degree of estrangement. The Christian story teaches us to see every human being as "one for whom Christ died" (Rom. 14:15), one sought by God's mercy and intended for friendship with God. Each one is precious to God and therefore has a claim on our attention and our care.

It is harder to think in terms of "us" and "them," harder at least to justify marking off some people as outside the sphere of our concern when the central story of our community is about how God sets out to reconcile humankind to God and to one another. According to that story, no human being can be merely a stranger to another, for we are all joined by having one need, one hope, one future bought for us by the quintessential Stranger on Earth: Jesus. What is more, proclaiming and embodying that hope is the very purpose for which the church exists. When St. Paul writes to the troubled Corinthian church to defend the source and authority of his ministry, he sums it up like this: "God was in Christ reconciling the world to himself, and entrusting to us the message of reconciliation" (2 Cor. 5:19). This is the hallmark and test of authentically Christian teaching.

Finally, Christian faith gives us some particular resources for guiding and sustaining the hard practical work of compassion that the love of neighbor undertakes. In affirming that God's good future for the world will ultimately prevail, such faith offers hope to counter the despair that can paralyze us. It offers the notion of vocation, a calling that matches our gifts to God's work in the world, and so engages each of us in a task that is vital without being overwhelming.

At the same time, the Christian insistence that God alone is Lord and Redeemer provides a limit to human ambition, even our ambition to rescue the world. This is a check on the dangerous zeal for fixing society that has sometimes led reformers to run roughshod over actual human beings for the sake of humanity in the abstract. The things Christians believe help nerve them for the long, patient work of doing what can be done to help, even when what can be done is no more than keeping company with those who mourn.

MADE INTO NEIGHBORS

Important as they are, however, the doctrines of Christian faith alone are not enough to change how we see and experience one another. Even for those who genuinely embrace such commitments, they do not necessarily open our eyes or our hearts to love all those whom God sends our way. It takes more than new ideas to change the way we see; it takes a new experience, and transformation is more likely to come from what we do than from what we think. We learn to love our neighbors by serving in some practical fashion the neighbor who confronts us, no matter how we feel at the outset.

In part this conclusion comes out of my observations over many years as a teacher of Christian youth and adults. All the preaching and teaching in the world about the plight of the suffering or the duty of Christians to respond does not have as much impact as one mission trip to build a school or staff a clinic or even just to companion those whose lives have been devastated by some disaster. The same conclusion has been reached by many others. This realization is reflected in the practice that is becoming more and more common of having students at Christian colleges and seminaries complete a significant term of social service as part of their education. It is true, certainly, that we are moved to help those we love. But it is also true that we are moved to love those we help, those whose humanity and dignity we confront along with their need.

The same lesson is taught by Christian history and in an example that is among my favorite stories of conversion. John Wesley, the founder of Methodism, was an eighteenth-century

Anglican priest. He had been raised in a strict and pious home and educated at Oxford University to take his place in the leadership of the Church of England. Two experiences converged that changed the expected course of his life, and with it the shape of Protestant faith in England and America. One experience was that he wrestled and finally came to terms with his own intolerable sense of falling short of the demand of God's holiness. Wesley came to absorb deeply the fundamental message of the Reformation: that the favor of God is not the *result* of any goodness of ours but is instead the *cause* of it. All our obedience is simply the reliable sign of grace already at work, a response to the gift already given freely in Jesus. Wesley's personal sense of being set free from fear and guilt by the mercy of God made him a powerful evangelist, one who used to ride in the cart with the condemned on the way to the gallows to offer them the boundless and saving grace of Jesus. The second experience that reshaped Wesley's career was his lifelong work with the poor and despised of England, those overlooked and crushed by the Industrial Revolution just rising in his day.

According to his own account, Wesley began this service as a young man in the least promising way possible. He had read of the wrath of God that threatened those who had "seen [Jesus] hungry and not fed [him] or thirsty and not given [him] drink" (Matt. 25:42). At this time, still striving to be good enough to win God's approval, Wesley set out to help the poor because he was afraid not to, and for no better reason. It is also likely that he began with all the comfortable prejudices of any eighteenth-century English gentleman about the lower classes, convinced of the vices that made them poor and the path of virtue that could lead them out of poverty if only they would improve.

But Wesley did not merely make a donation to the benevolence fund and go on thinking of the poor as he had before. Taking Jesus at his word about meeting him in the suffering, he went to the sick and the hungry and offered his service in person, and he kept coming. He went back to cottage and workhouse and prison, back to field and coal mine and shanty to bring preaching and instruction, food and medicine, blankets and clothing to the desperate. And along the way he learned: of the appalling conditions and the outright abuse and corruption suffered by the working class, of the grinding misery but also of the strength and resilience of the destitute.

As a minister of the gospel, Wesley did not just provide desperately needed help. He invited these people into the challenge and dignity of discipleship. He taught and was taught by them, until his heart and his vision were transformed and he knew these people for God's own. In the end he came to prefer their company and the seriousness of their struggle for faith and faithfulness amid hardships to the genteel and superficial piety of his own class. After a stint as a visiting preacher in a wealthy congregation he wrote in his journal, "How hard it is to be shallow enough for a polite audience!"[4] Because John Wesley obeyed the call to care for the suffering, prejudices and mixed motives and all, he made neighbors out of strangers and was made a true neighbor to them in turn. By this the path was opened for them to become brothers and sisters.

CONCEIVING THE LOVE OF ENEMIES

Hard as the love of strangers may be, it is easy in comparison to the final test of neighbor love, the love of enemies. When we set aside the fact that it is so familiar a part of Christian teaching, the command that we are to love our enemies seems very nearly absurd. It sounds to us like a contradiction in terms, and we will do better to begin by owning up to our perplexity than by pretending we understand what this *means,* much less how we should do it or why. I suspect the only reason we are not more offended by this teaching is that we don't take it seriously enough.

By definition, enemies are people we fear and distrust. They are those who would do us harm, those against whom we must, at a minimum, defend ourselves. This much seems to be common sense. In addition, enemies may include those who have wronged us so deeply, so irreparably, that we actively want to harm them in turn, even if only to make sure they don't hurt us again. How would it even be possible to love them? Surely we cannot wish them success, not when their aim may be to destroy us. We cannot feel warmly toward them or rejoice to find them in our world, because they intend us harm or have already done it. We cannot enjoy them or be grateful for them or even (sometimes) leave off condemning them in the strongest possible terms. What kind of love could make sense despite all that?

The answer given by Christian tradition has always been that what we aim for, and what we need, is a love like God's. Of course we have already seen that Christians trace all human loves to their source in God and make divine love the touchstone and standard for all that counts as genuine love. But in the love of enemies we come to the furthest reaches of human possibility, where nothing short of the direct imitation of God will carry us. We now have to try and understand something about God's love for enemies, what it does and doesn't require, and how it might transform us if we were willing.

To begin with, we have to distinguish between two things we often confuse, which are love and something like approval. We blend these two things naturally enough because so many of our ordinary human loves include approval and are based on it. They spring from admiration or from appreciation or from gratitude. In our loves of friendship or romance or affection, the things that spark love are also things worthy of praise. They are part of the goodness we see in the other person, and delight in.

But when Jesus commends the love of enemies, he expressly sets gratitude and mutual affection aside. "If you love those who love you, what reward do you deserve? Even the tax collectors do that much. If you warmly greet only your brothers and sisters, what is remarkable about that? Unbelievers do that too" (Matt. 5:46–47 AT). Instead he tells them, "Love your enemies, and pray for those who persecute you. . . . Only so can you be children of your Father in heaven, who causes the sun to shine on good and evil alike, and sends rain on the just and the unjust" (Matt. 5:44 AT).

It is important to see that God's kindness toward wrongdoers, the provision of the basic resources of sun and rain (the very sources of life in an agricultural society), does not have anything to do with approval or with wishing them success in their wrongdoing. To speak of people as good and evil, just and unjust, is hardly to say that these distinctions are not real or do not matter. Certainly Jesus does not suggest that it does not matter which one you are.

Instead, the whole point of the text is that God's own holiness is the standard for Jesus' followers, so the passage ends with a breathtaking call to his disciples: "You must be perfect, as your Father in heaven is perfect" (Matt. 5:48 AT). What Jesus says is not that God is indifferent to evil but just that *goodness is not a precondition for being loved by God,* who is "kind to the selfish and ungrateful" (Luke 6:35). So goodness is not to be a condition for our love either.

Loving enemies as God loves them would have to mean sustaining their lives and hoping for the best for them. Paul, who seems here to be reflecting this same teaching of Jesus, makes the instruction explicit in Romans: "If your enemies are hungry, feed them; if they are thirsty, give them something to drink" (12:20). But loving those who have made themselves God's enemies by injustice would also have to include willing that they would be transformed, even for their own sakes. What is best for wrongdoers, after all, is to repent and be reconciled to God and other people.

This means that the love of enemies is not naïve or sentimental, and it can have real teeth. Here is how Paul finishes his sentence about providing food and clothing to enemies: "for by doing this you will heap burning coals upon their heads." (If you have ever been on the receiving end of real kindness from someone you have deeply wronged, you will know just what he means here.) Paul is hoping by mercy to sear the consciences of the offenders. So the love he commends is perfectly compatible with trying to bring about a change.

What this love is not compatible with is the desire for revenge, for inflicting punishment the purpose of which is to make your enemies suffer, perhaps as you have suffered. Deep in us as the desire for retribution may be, the exacting of "an eye for an eye" is not how God has treated us, and Paul follows

Jesus in forbidding it: "Return no one evil for evil" (Rom. 12:17). But this does not mean that justice is simply foregone. To those who look for just punishment, Paul says, "Beloved, never avenge yourselves, but leave it to the wrath of God" (Rom. 12:19). Justice that is true, impartial, and genuine is in God's keeping, and we know from the long witness of scripture that God's wrath is set against all that destroys life and rends the peace of Creation. Yet God still loves and yearns after those who have been enemies, as Jesus in his teaching and ultimately in his death bears witness. We will be God's children if we are willing to love as God loves.

TRANSFORMING DESIRE

Here we run into a kind of roadblock, which is that (frankly) we're *not* willing. Of course, we may be sufficiently struck by the power and beauty of Jesus' picture of unconditional love to be moved by it. (This is suggested by the fact that the Sermon on the Mount, in spite of all its astonishing demands, remains high on the list of favorite Bible passages of people the world over.) But when it comes to acting according to Jesus' teaching, we quickly find that we don't really want closeness to God on these terms, or enough to pay this kind of price.

Many years ago I sent my three-year-old daughter into her room with instructions to pick up the toys she had left scattered from one end of it to the other. I came to check on her ten or fifteen minutes later and was surprised to find her sitting contentedly on the floor playing with something, the toys still scattered and the toy box still empty. I asked her with some irritation why she had not picked up any of her toys and she answered me with remarkable clarity: "I can't want to," she said.

I was struck by the perfect exactness of her response. She hadn't picked up her toys because she didn't want to, even though she knew she was supposed to do it. At three she did not yet have the capacity to do what she was supposed to in spite of not wanting to, at least not without help. Neither did she know how to change her desires. So she just went back to doing what came naturally.

I thought at the time that we were all in exactly the same position. Often we may know what we ought to do but we do not want to do it; sometimes we can't even imagine wanting to. Never is the chasm between what we ought to do and what we want greater than when we confront the seeming impossibility of loving our enemies. We have no idea how to transform our own wills so that we can love as God loves and act as Jesus commands. Unable to do as we are bidden, we fall back on what comes naturally: as in the popular proverb Jesus quotes (Matt. 5:43), we love our friends and hate our enemies.

Through all of this we may see and be drawn by the beauty of God's all-embracing love. We may even realize that we ourselves are dependent on that same patient and forgiving love that, as Paul reminds us, came to seek and reconcile us while we were yet enemies (Rom. 5:10). We may know too that we are called to respond in kind, to love one another as Jesus has loved us. But we "can't want to." To imitate such a love is too costly, and too frightening. We too will need help—help that can change not only what we do but also what we desire.

Becoming able to love our enemies requires in some ways the opposite of learning to love the neighbors who confront us as strangers. There we are standing at a distance, with no emotional connection to these other people. In our relation to strangers, our temptation is to remain simply indifferent and unaffected by our neighbors' need, and the challenge is to come close enough to let ourselves be moved. But in our encounters with our enemies we are anything but indifferent. Instead of standing too far away, we are standing too near; we are too much affected by our anger and our fear, too much a part of the picture to see it with any perspective. We are doing well if we can see our enemies fairly and truthfully; to see them with compassion or charity is more than we can manage. So what we need is a kind of distance, a degree of disengagement from the conflict that lets our passions cool and helps us see from a standpoint not our own.

PRAYING FOR THE ENEMY

I suspect that this need for a change in perspective, more than anything, is the reason Jesus immediately follows the command to love your enemies with the instruction to pray for them (Matt. 5:44). The purpose of these prayers is not to change our enemies, and even less to change God's mind about what should happen. It is to change *us*: what we can see in the situation and what we can hope for, what we fear and what we want, so that we may finally change what we are able to do.

Now, I would not be surprised if most of our prayers for our enemies started out as really prayers *about* them (prayers that they would stop doing whatever has made them our enemies) and prayers *for* us (for example, that God would keep them from doing us harm). There is nothing wrong with prayers like these, especially if we really have been the victims of some kind of serious and unprovoked assault. (The Psalms include many such prayers.) But we are not yet on the path that would lead us to the love of enemies. For that we have to take another step, one that is far harder. We have to ask God to bless those whom we fear and wish to hate.

I do not want to minimize the difficulty or the strangeness of such a prayer. It requires that we do something that feels like abandoning our own skin: that we stand alongside Jesus and ask God's kindness for those who may be seeking our lives. It means that we have to put aside all our claims, the just along with the unjust, to lay down our anger and our desire for revenge. It asks us to trade our own causes for God's cause, which is the reclaiming of the world through mercy.

Though it is the same mercy shown to us in Jesus Christ, the same mercy on which we all depend, nevertheless in my slender experience it does not come to us naturally. We may have to ask for help even to frame the words, and considerably more help ever to begin to mean them. Here is where Christians invoke the aid of the Holy Spirit to enable us to pray as we ought. But this is also where we begin to offer our enemies along with ourselves to God, so that God's reign may come and God's good purposes be fulfilled.

If prayer is the crucial turn toward loving our enemies, it must be acknowledged that such prayer takes time, perhaps a whole lifetime, to learn. It also takes a community. We need a community of others to challenge and support us in rejecting the common sense of retaliation, and to model the thousand small acts of patience and forbearance by which we learn to practice forgiveness and charity toward one another. It is also in communities of faith, where the love of neighbor is practiced and the truth is spoken, that we come to see just how much forbearance we ourselves require from those who love us, and how little true justice any of us could bear. There we may even learn to question the perfect justness of our own most cherished causes.

It was from the community I serve that, on a morning five years ago, I learned my most powerful lesson about the love of enemies. It was a bright blue morning near the start of the school year and I was driving in to campus for a 9:00 meeting when I heard on the radio the first report of a plane striking the World Trade Center tower. It did not even occur to me that it was anything but a terrible accident, and I arrived early and went inside before anything more was broadcast. When I got into our meeting room I told the half-dozen of my colleagues gathered there what I had heard, and we stopped to wonder and silently pray before we turned to the business at hand. It was perhaps thirty minutes later that a missing member of the committee arrived, looking utterly white, and told us that he had just seen a jetliner fly into the side of the Pentagon.

Like every other adult in the country, I remember a great deal about that day in September 2001: where I was when I first understood what had happened, what I saw and thought and felt, the people I called and those I could not reach for hours on end. But more than anything else, I remember and am grateful for the people I was privileged to be with and for what I saw happen among them that day.

I am not even sure how it came about that the whole community converged in the chapel a little later that morning. Perhaps someone officially called for a time of community prayer and worship, or perhaps it was just that in our seminary the chapel is where people go when they are in trouble or in pain. There was no particular order and no plan. The president of the seminary opened with prayer and simply invited all to speak as they were moved. Most of us, too numb for words of our own, prayed aloud psalms or read scripture passages that affirmed God's sustaining presence in the face of disaster and death.

It was a powerful but also a terribly painful time. In my Washington, D.C., school, dozens of our students and staff had parents or spouses or children who worked in the Pentagon, and many of our student pastors had congregants who worked there. For many hours there was effectively no working phone service in the city, and families had to wait through much of the day to learn whether the people they loved were safe. The pain and fear were almost palpable, and throughout our time together the sound of weeping could be heard as people held each other and shared their grief and terror.

That morning we prayed together texts rarely heard in church: the psalms of lament and even the terrible psalms of imprecation that call down God's wrath on the wicked. Through them we acknowledged before God our anger and our desire that justice would be done to those who had planned such wholesale and indiscriminate slaughter, even that they should suffer as they had made others suffer.

We were together a long time, and in truth it took a long time but eventually something changed. From the rawness of shock and the readiness of our cries for retribution there emerged, painfully and fearfully, the beginnings of other prayers. Someone prayed to understand what had brought about this tragedy, to fathom what had given birth to such rage and hatred and despair. Someone else prayed for patience and restraint on the part of our leaders, that our nation would not rush to judgment and to retaliation. And then some brave soul, I do not know who, prayed that God would give us hearts like Jesus' heart, that we might be brought to forgive those who had done us such terrible harm, and that we might resist our desire to return evil for evil. The silence after that was long. And finally, finally, we prayed for those who had done these terrible things, that God would have mercy on them.

That was almost too much for us that morning, I admit, and I am sure there were some in the sanctuary who could not join in such a prayer. But it was held out before us even on that first terrible day. It was presented to our imaginations as a form that Christian faithfulness might take, and that alone was extraordinary. And before we left the chapel, we managed to pray together the prayer that Jesus taught the disciples, including that God would forgive our sins as we forgave those who sinned against us. In all the days and months that followed, through all the struggles of the nation and the Church to come to terms with what had happened and how we should respond, it was those hours of wrenching but transforming communal prayer that grounded us. They kept us looking for an answer better, truer, and more faithful than revenge.

However, one point has to be made clear. To pray for God's best for an enemy does not mean that the world is abandoned to injustice, as if the only possible resistance to evil is to be found in hatred and violence and the endless cycles of retaliation to which they give rise. It hardly needs to be pointed out that this, the world's perennial strategy, has had little success in bringing about justice and peace in the world. When Paul advises his Church to bless and not to curse their persecutors, he ends with this instruction: "Do not be overcome by evil, but overcome evil with good" (12:21). The love of enemies *is* God's strategy for restoring Creation, and what Christians affirm is that hidden in the cross is the victory that overcomes the world.

But honesty compels me to say one thing more, something that anyone who dares to hold up the love of enemies as a serious call must acknowledge: The victory claimed by the cross is hidden, deeply hidden, in a world that to all appearances is still ruled by force and fear. No one who tells the story Christians tell can pretend that gentleness toward enemies will always, or even often, bring about their conversion. Jesus, after all, died. He was not rescued but resurrected, and only confidence in that central Christian claim can make sense of following him on the path he walked. As popular as the idea has become that Jesus was not divine but was nevertheless a great moral teacher, it falls apart when it comes to this: if Jesus was wrong about who he was and what God was doing in the world through him, then his moral advice about the love of enemies amounts to suicide. As Paul said, "If only for this life have we hoped in Christ, then we are of all people most to be pitied" (1 Cor. 15:19).

This means that everything I have been laying out in this book—the Christian understanding of love as the heart and center of a life worth living, its insistence that God is the source of all true loves and the test of what counts as love—all depends on the truth of something that cannot be demonstrated. The letter to the Hebrews calls faith "the assurance of things hoped for, and the conviction of things not seen" (11:1). To walk the path sketched throughout these pages, to model our loves on the love of God, and to practice the disciplines of Christian life as means of learning to love well and faithfully—all of these are acts of faith. They depend on the conviction of things unseen. They represent a bet that God is real, a wager that love and not violence ultimately rules the universe, and the stakes are in truth not less than everything. But the vision promised to those who make such a wager is glorious: "Blessed are the merciful, for they shall obtain mercy. Blessed are the peacemakers, for they shall be called the children of God. Blessed are the pure in heart, for they shall see God" (Matt. 5:7, 9; 5:8).

NOTES

CHAPTER ONE

1. Most of the Bible verses quoted in this volume are from the New Revised Standard Version. Exceptions are marked RSV for *Revised Standard Version,* KJV for the *King James Version,* NIV for the *Holy Bible New International Version,* or AT for texts translated directly by the author.
2. For a convenient and illuminating introduction to the setting and situation of 1 John, see the essay on 1 John in the *Oxford Bible Commentary,* John Barton and John Muddiman, eds. (New York: Oxford University Press, 2001), 1274–1281.
3. Citations are so numerous it would be tedious to list them all. For examples, see Matt. 5:43–44; Rom. 12:14–21; James 2:8–14; and 1 John 3:17–18.

CHAPTER TWO

1. *Sayings of the Desert Fathers,* trans. Benedicta Ward (Kalamazoo, MI: Cistercian Publications, 1975), 57.
2. Thomas Merton, *New Seeds of Contemplation* (New York: New Directions, 1961), 7.
3. David Myers, *The Pursuit of Happiness* (San Francisco: Harper-Collins, 1996).
4. It is Christopher Lasch's *Haven in a Heartless World: The Family Besieged* (New York: Basic Books, 1977) that made this phrase famous.

5. Nygren's work appears in English in *Agape and Eros,* trans. Philip Watson (New York: HarperCollins, 1963).

6. Ibid., 129.

7. Dietrich Bonhoeffer, *Life Together: A Discussion of Christian Fellowship* (New York: HarperCollins, 1954).

8. Ibid., 23.

9. Ibid., 31.

10. Ibid., 31.

11. Ibid., 33.

12. Ibid., 34.

13. Ibid., 35.

14. Ibid., 38.

CHAPTER THREE

1. Remarks of William Oglesby, from class notes, Family Counseling, Union Theological Seminary, Virginia, Spring 1981.

2. There are, however, people to whom jealousy seems to be proof that they are really loved, as though being possessed were the only alternative to being unwanted.

3. H. Richard Niebuhr, *The Purpose of the Church and Its Ministry* (New York: HarperCollins, 1956), 35. Italics added.

4. For a more extensive but still very accessible discussion, see Walter Brueggemann's article "The Liturgy of Abundance, the Myth of Scarcity" in *Christian Century,* Mar. 24–31, 1999, *116*(10), 342–347.

5. This was Martin Luther's reply to the papal delegate who threatened him with arrest, imprisonment, and execution for teaching contrary to Catholic doctrine.

CHAPTER FOUR

1. An interesting look at this phenomenon in American society from the standpoint of sociology is Robert B. Putnam's *Bowling Alone* (New York: Simon and Schuster, 2000).

2. Gilbert Meilaender, *Friendship: A Study in Theological Ethics* (Notre Dame, IN: Notre Dame University Press, 1981), 104.

3. The standard source for this understanding is Aristotle's treatise on friendship in Books VIII and IX of the *Nicomachean Ethics*. It says a great deal about the significance attached to this kind of love that it was deemed an appropriate subject for philosophical reflection, as an aspect of the good life.

4. Here the seminal source is Aelrad of Rivealux, *Spiritual Friendship*, trans. Mary Eugenia Lake SSND (Washington, DC: Cistercian Publications, 1974).

5. G. K. Chesterton, *St. Francis of Assisi* (New York: Continuum, 2001), 1–10.

6. Jim Jones was the leader of a group that began as a church and over time became a cult of personality. He eventually led his followers to found a settlement in Guyana, where he became more domineering and the settlement became more reclusive as Jones descended further into paranoia. In 1978 he led his people in a mass suicide in which 916 people died.

7. This account of love as dependent on vision is indebted to Margaret Farley's discussion in *Personal Commitments: Making, Keeping, Changing* (San Francisco: HarperCollins, 1986), 38–53. To her insights and to her suggestions for how the vision of love might be recovered we will return later.

8. This is the counterpoint to Bonhoeffer's claim, noted in Chapter Two, that the willingness to surrender the beloved is what distinguishes spiritual from merely human love.

9. I was told this story by one of the close ministry colleagues of the Baptist minister. The pastor wishes to remain unidentified.

10. Some reflections on this problem can be found in the accounts of the Mississippi Summer of 1964. See, for example, Adam Fairclough's *Better Day Coming* (New York: Viking Penguin, 2001), 281–286.

CHAPTER FIVE

1. Harville Hendrix, *Getting the Love You Want* (New York: Holt, 2001).

2. Joel Osteen, *Your Best Life Now* (New York: Warner Books, 2005). No particular comment on the contents of this volume is intended,

since I have not read it. I note merely that the approach appeals to self-fulfillment.

3. Brilliant (and disturbing) examples of such parodies can be seen in surprising places, including such animated shows for adults as *The Simpsons* and *Family Guy,* both on Fox Television.

4. For a convenient summary of some of these data, see J. Wallerstein, J. M. Lewis, and S. Blakeslee, *The Unexpected Legacy of Divorce* (New York: Hyperion Books, 2000).

5. The studies to support these generalizations are easy to find. Here is a small sample:

About work hours, see Edward Prescott, "Why Do Americans Work So Much More Than Europeans?" *Federal Reserve Bank Quarterly Review,* 2004, *28*(1), 2–13.

On reduced sleeping time, see http://www.sleepfoundation.org/_content/hottopics/2005_summary_of_findings.pdf.

Regarding diet, see "Dietary Trends, American," available at http://www.faqs.org/nutrition/Diab-Em/Dietary-Trends-American.html; or "Food Surveys Research Group: What We Eat in America" at http://www.barc.usda.gov/bhnrc/foodsurvey. Compounding the problem, according to surveys done by the Health and Human Services Department, is the fact that seven out of ten Americans do not get regular exercise, and 62 percent report never engaging in vigorous physical activity lasting as long as ten minutes. See Margaret Lethbridge-Cejku, Deborah Rose, and Jackline Vickerie, "Summary Health Statistics for U.S. Adults: National Health Interview Survey, 2004,"VHS 10:228 (Hyattsville, MD: National Center for Health Statistics, 2006).

On greater social isolation, see Robert D. Putnam, *Bowling Alone* (New York: Simon and Schuster, 2001); and Miller McPherson, Lynn Smith-Lovin, and Matthew E. Brashears, "Social Isolation in America: Changes in Core Discussion Networks over Two Decades," *American Sociological Review,* 2006, *71,* 353–375.

6. See, for example, Luther's classic treatise *The Freedom of a Christian,* available on-line at http://ctsfw.edu/etext/luther/freedom.

7. *The Confessions of St. Augustine,* Book I, chap. vii, para. 11. Many translations of the Confessions are in the public domain, and they can be printed or read online for free. An excellent example is Albert Outler's translation available at http://www.ccel.org/ccel/augustine/confessions/confessions.html.

8. *City of God,* Book 19, chap. 28.

9. Ibid.

10. *Confessions,* Book I, chap. i, para. 1.

11. *Confessions,* Book II, chap. ii, para. 2.

12. *Confessions,* Book II, chap. ix, para. 17.

13. "Being rich toward God"(Luke 12:21) is a traditional phrase for almsgiving in the wisdom literature of the Old Testament.

14. David Yeago, Lutheran Theological Southern Seminary, South Carolina, private conversation.

15. Lady Bountiful is a character in the 1707 comedy *Beaux' Stratagem* by playwright George Farquhar (1678–1707).

CHAPTER SIX

1. Margaret A. Farley, *Personal Commitments: Making, Keeping, Changing* (San Francisco: HarperCollins, 1986).

2. Ibid., 58ff.

3. As this way of putting it suggests, a partner's unwillingness to remain in a marriage is one of the circumstances in which the New Testament seems to offer a ground for accepting divorce. There is much more to be said about the biblical view of marriage and divorce, and about implications of that view for Christians facing such decisions. For careful and extended discussions, see David Gushee, *Getting Marriage Right* (Grand Rapids, MI: Baker Books, 2004); and Richard Hays, *The Moral Vision of the New Testament* (San Francisco: HarperCollins, 1996), 347–375.

CHAPTER SEVEN

1. Gilbert Meilaender, *Friendship: A Study in Theological Ethics* (Notre Dame, IN: Notre Dame University Press, 1981), 54.

2. This story was told to me by the pastor, by then a man of middle age and many years' experience, as one of the most important lesson he ever learned in ministry.

3. This aspect of spiritual friendship has ancient roots, but this way of speaking of it is drawn from the early foundations of Methodism, my own theological tradition. It comes from John Wesley's "The Nature, Purpose, and General Rules of the Methodist Societies" and is one of the basic functions of the eighteenth-century class meetings that launched the Methodist movement.

4. I have related the story as well as I can in brief, but nothing is as wonderful as reading it in Augustine's own words. Many translations of the *Confessions* are in the public domain, and they can be downloaded or read online for free. The story is found in Book IV, chaps. 4–12.

5. *Confessions,* Book II, chap. 9, para. 17.

6. *Confessions,* Book IV, chap. 4, para. 9.

7. Ibid.

8. Ibid.

9. *Confessions,* Book IV, chap. 10, para. 15.

10. *Confessions,* Book IV, chap. 12, para. 18

11. *Confessions,* Book IV, chap. 8, para. 13.

12. *Confessions,* Book IV, chap. 9, para. 14.

CHAPTER EIGHT

1. The photographer was Steve McCurry and the image and the story associated with it can be reviewed on *National Geographic's* Website at http://www.nationalgeographic.com/ngm/100best/storyA_story.html.

2. To their credit, the publishers of *National Geographic* magazine have not only offered compensation to the subject of the photograph for use of her copyright-protected image but have also set up a foundation into which proceeds from its reproduction are deposited. The foundation provides funding for the education of Afghan girls.

3. The figure is based on the United Nations 2005 estimate of one malnutrition-related death every 3.6 seconds. See the UNICEF Millennium Development Goals Web page at http://www. unicef.org/mdg/poverty.html.

4. *Journal of John Wesley,* entry for August 25, 1771, in W. Reginald Ward and Richard Heitzenrater (eds.), *Journal and Diaries: Works of John Wesley,* Vol. 5 (Nashville, TN: Abingdon Press, 1993), 288.

THE AUTHOR

Sondra Wheeler grew up in Connecticut and was educated at Wesleyan University (B.A., 1979) and Yale University (M.A.R., 1987; Ph.D., 1992). After teaching at Duquesne University in Pittsburgh, she came to Washington, D.C., in 1993 to teach at Wesley Theological Seminary. There she is Martha Ashby Carr Professor of Christian Ethics and teaches bioethics, the history of theological ethics, and the virtue tradition as well as biblical ethics. She is author of *Wealth as Peril and Obligation: The New Testament on Possessions* (1995), *Stewards of Life: Bioethics and Pastoral Care* (1996), and a variety of articles on medical ethics as well as articles and contributions to edited volumes in other areas of theological ethics. She is presently at work on a fourth book about the moral relationship between parents and children. She lives in Maryland with her husband and son, and has grown daughters in New York and Philadelphia.

INDEX